50 Coloring Pages of Flowers : So Fun to Do

by Paula Roman-Leon and Rita Scafidi

50 Coloring Pages of Flowers : So Fun to Do

This is a work of non-fiction.

Illustrations copyrighted by Paula Roman-Leon and Rita Scafidi © 2021

Printed in the United States of America

A 2 Z Press LLC

PO Box 582

Deleon Springs, FL 32130

bestlittleonlinebookstore.com

sizemore3630@aol.com

440-241-3126

ISBN: 978-1-954191--52-5

DEDICATION

Paula dedicates this book to

Vladimir Roman-Leon

and

Rita dedicates this book to

my mom and dad,

I can't possibly thank you enough.

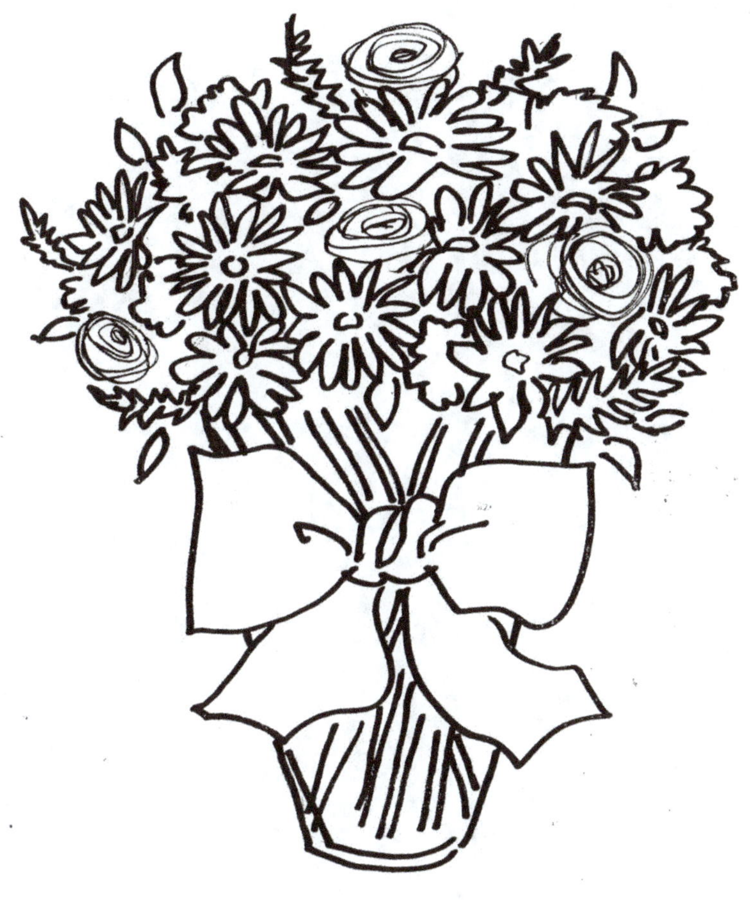

This book belongs to:

____

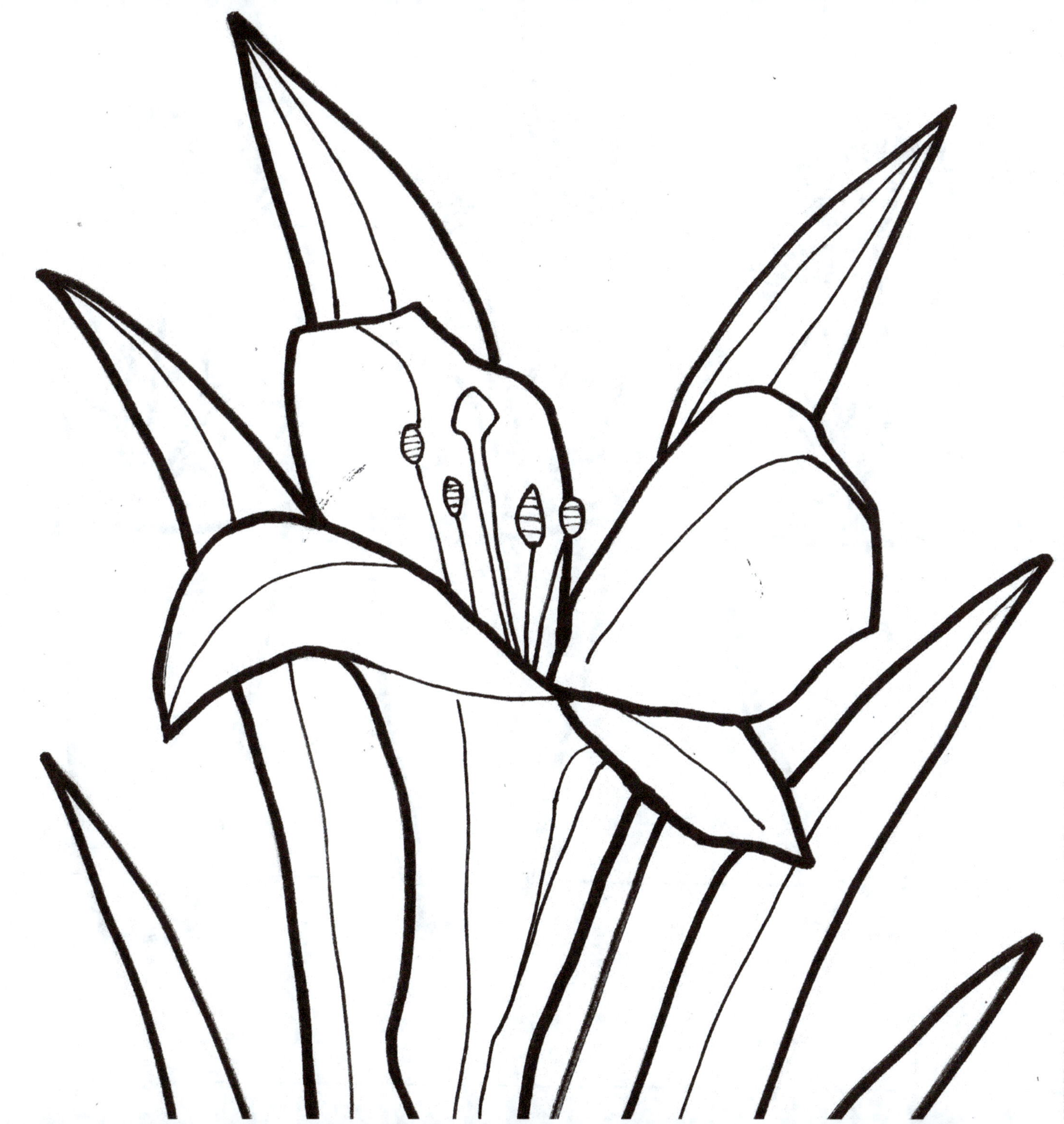

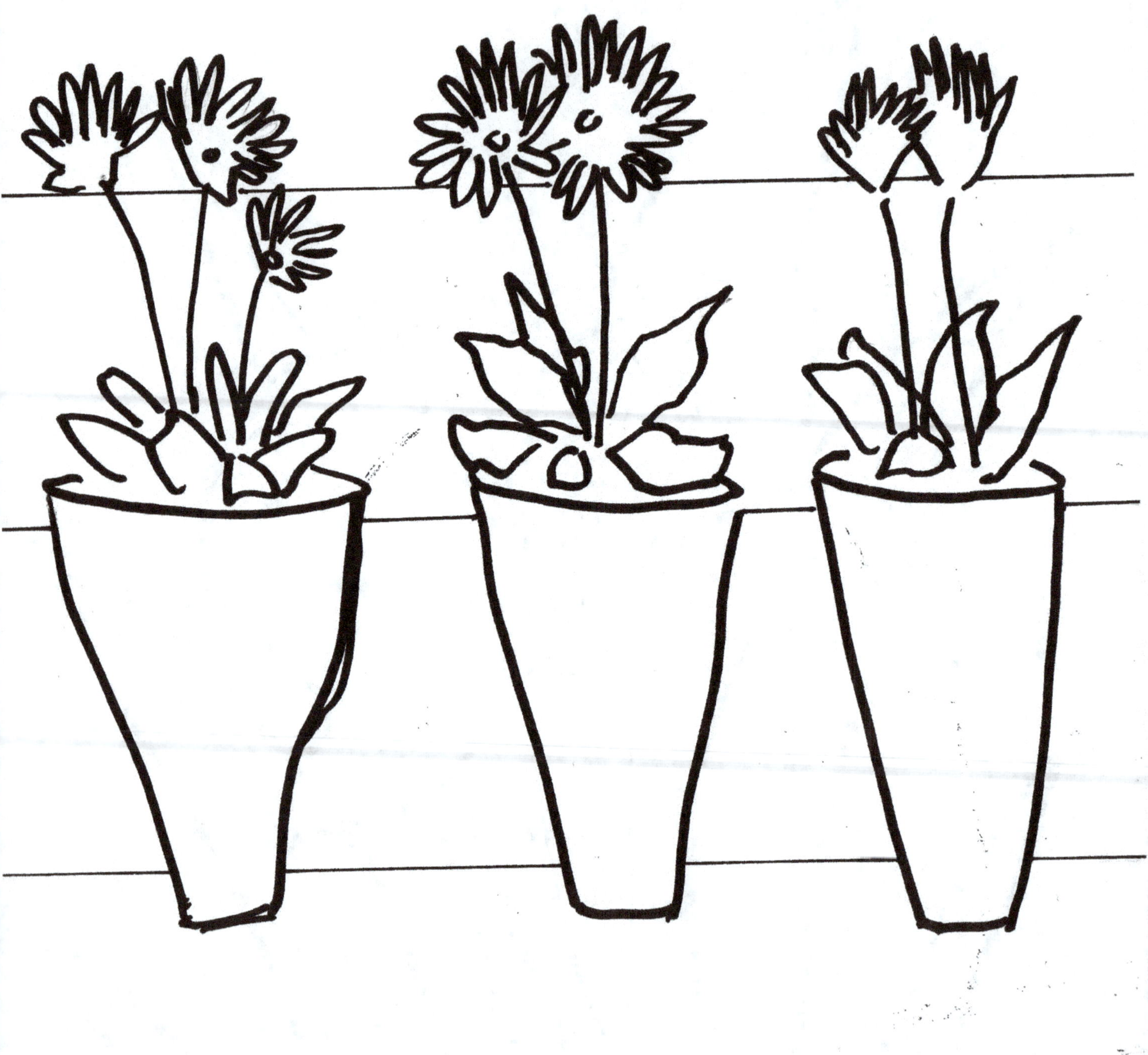

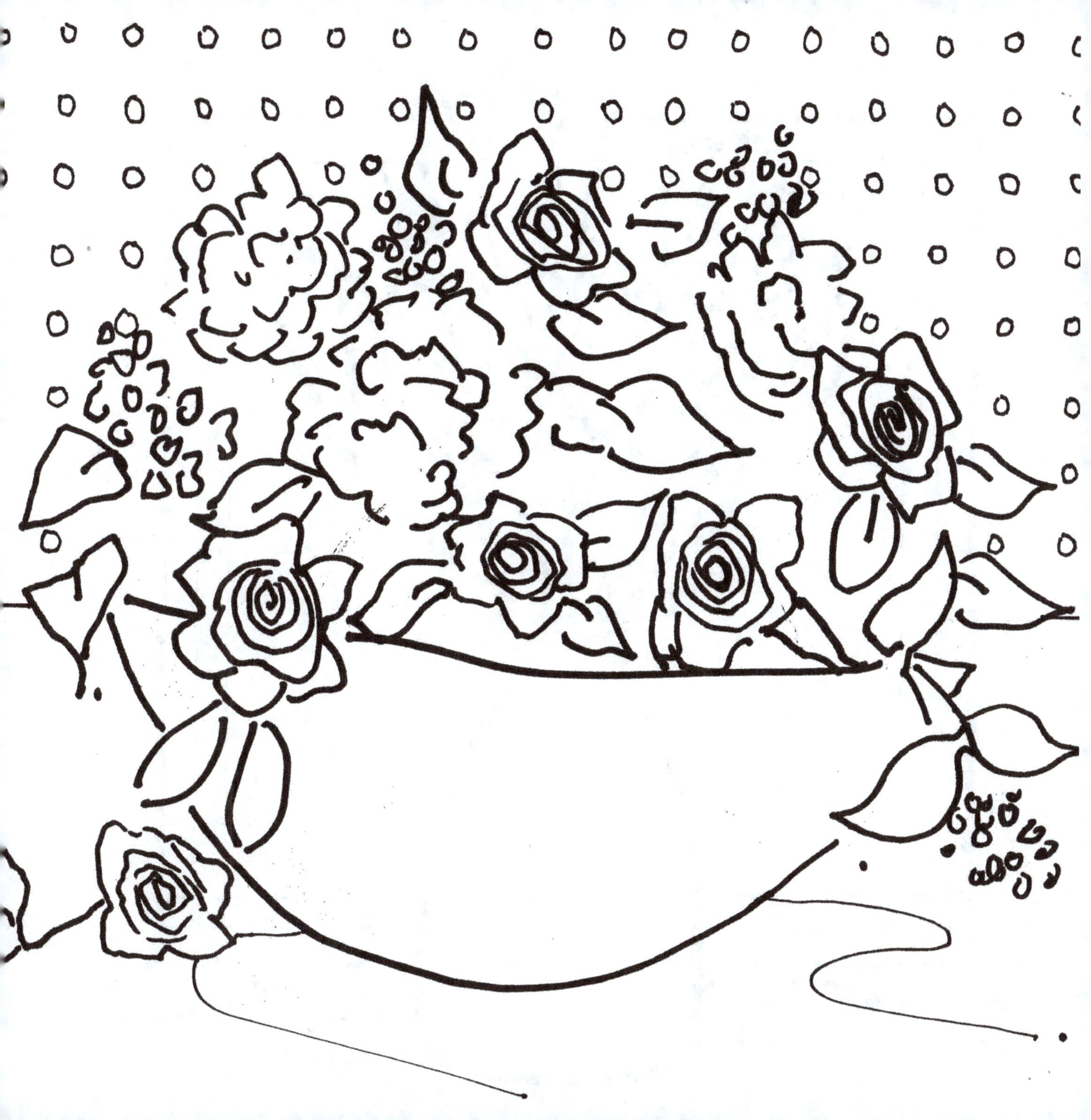

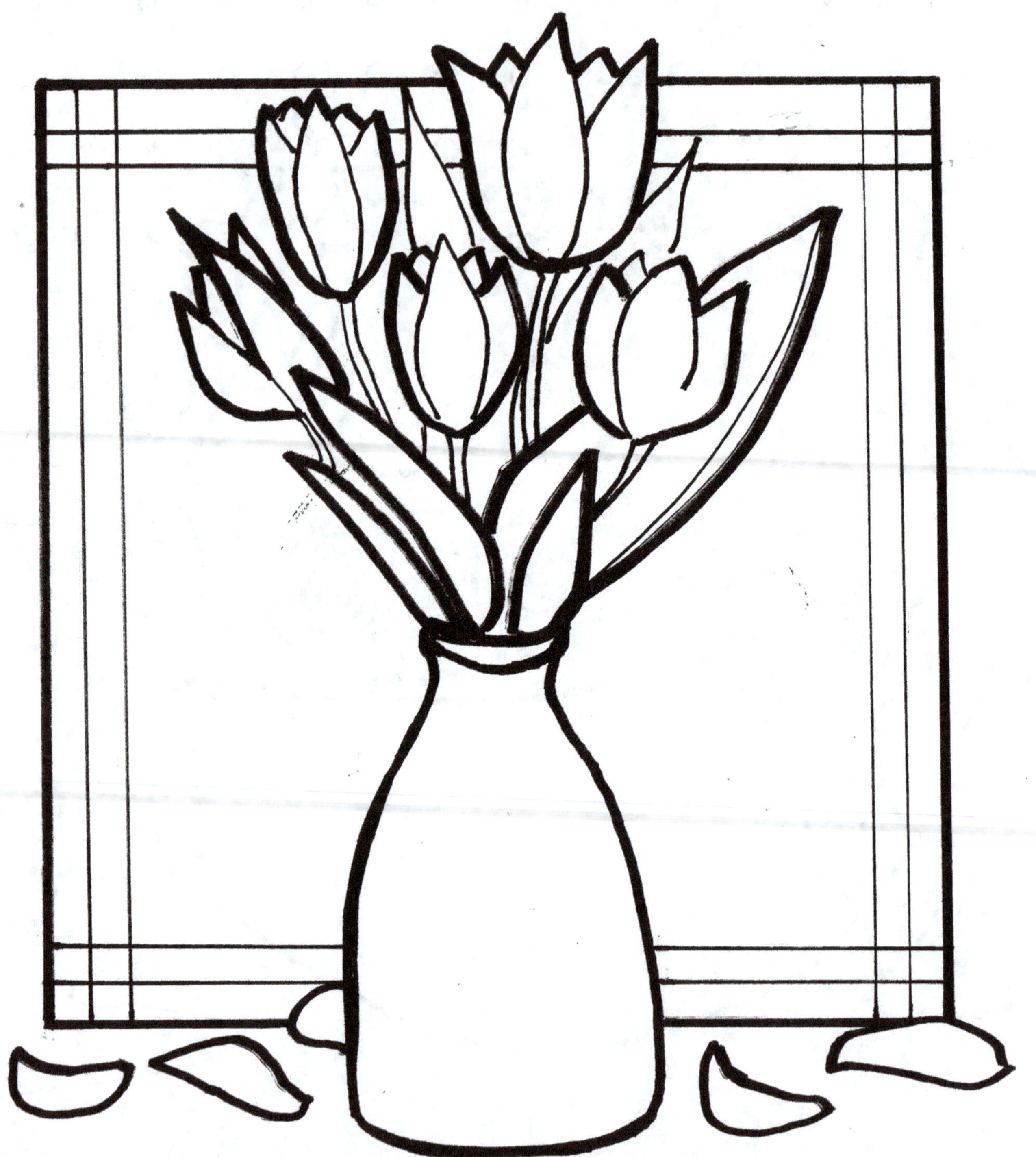

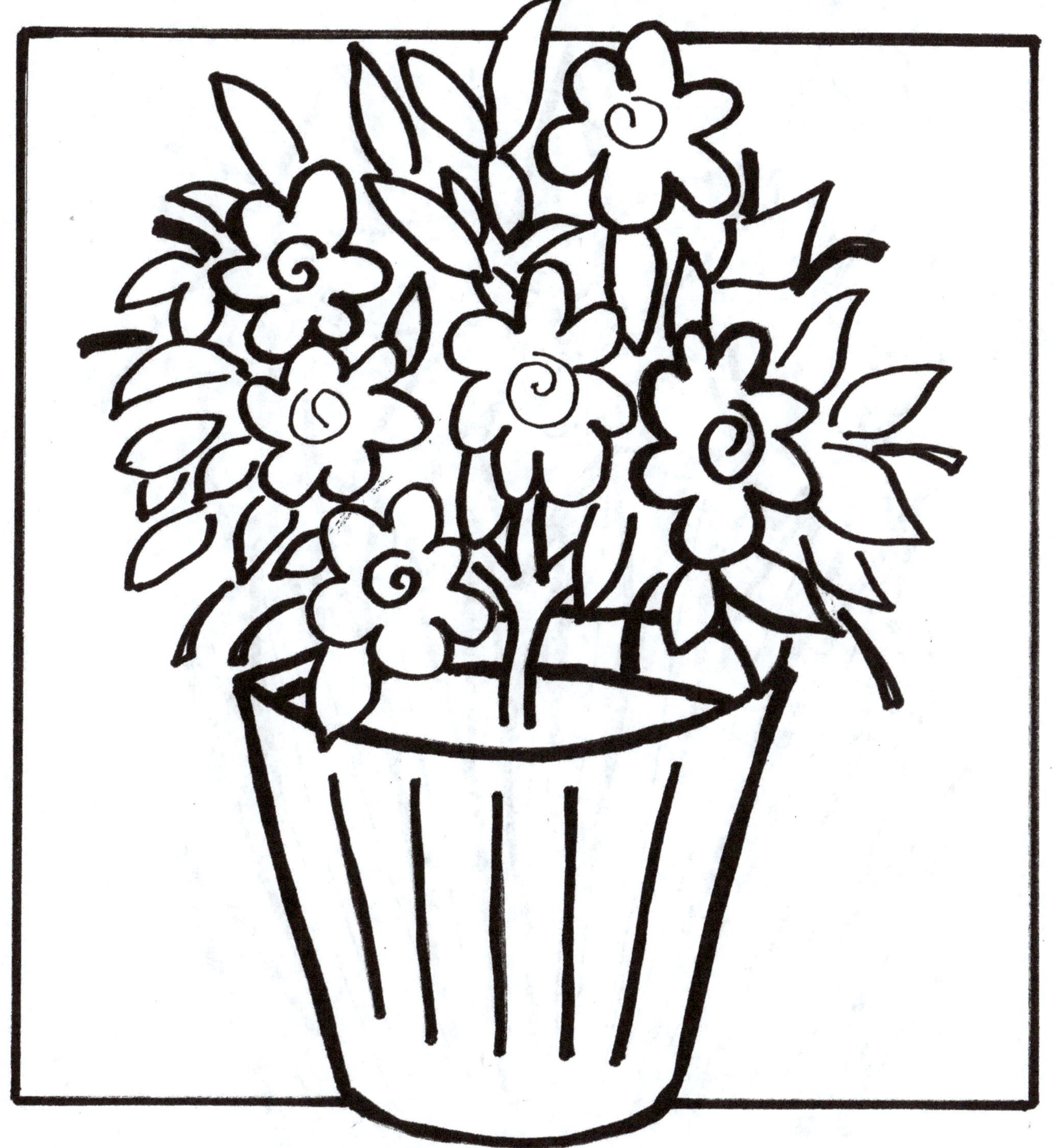

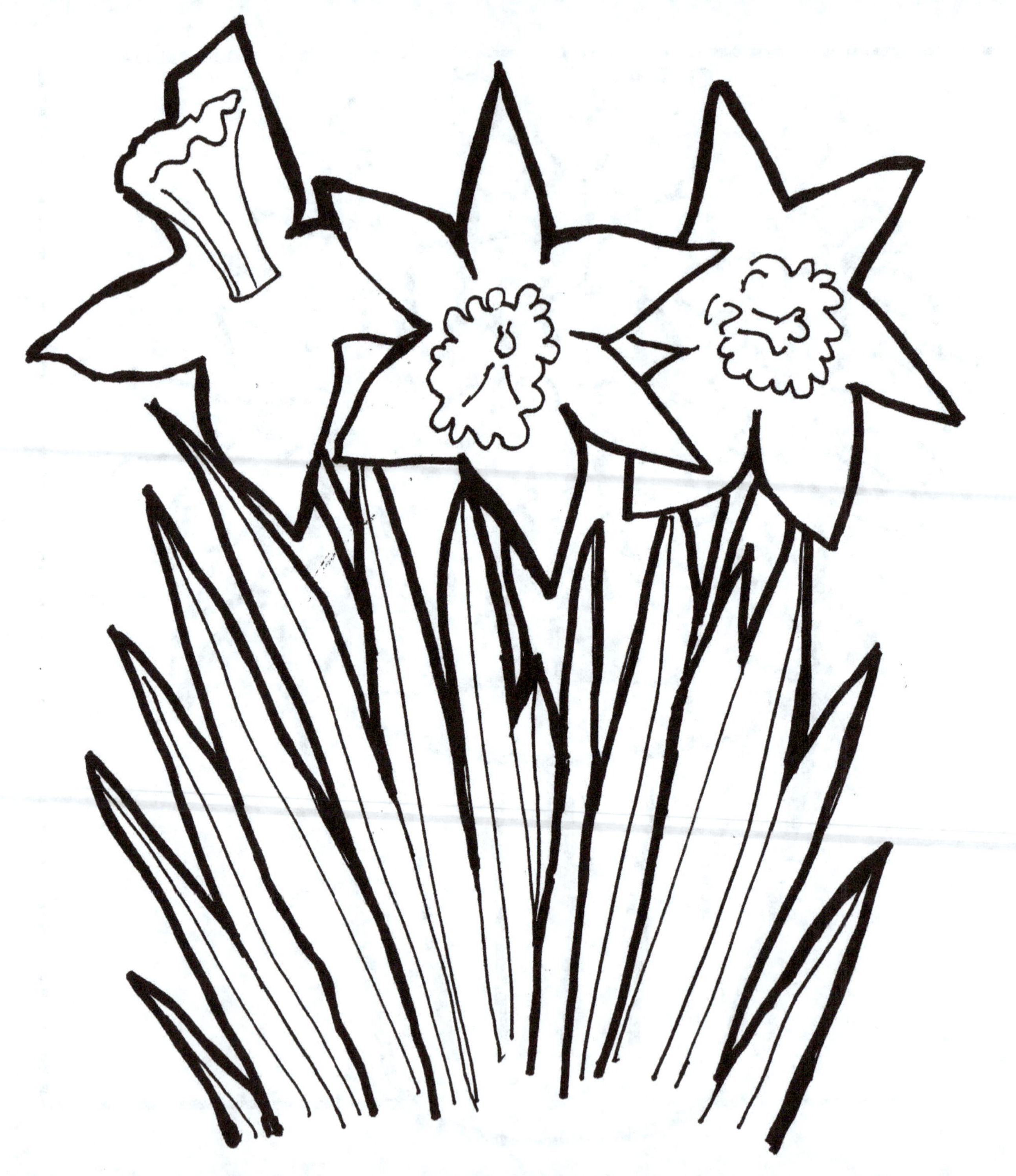

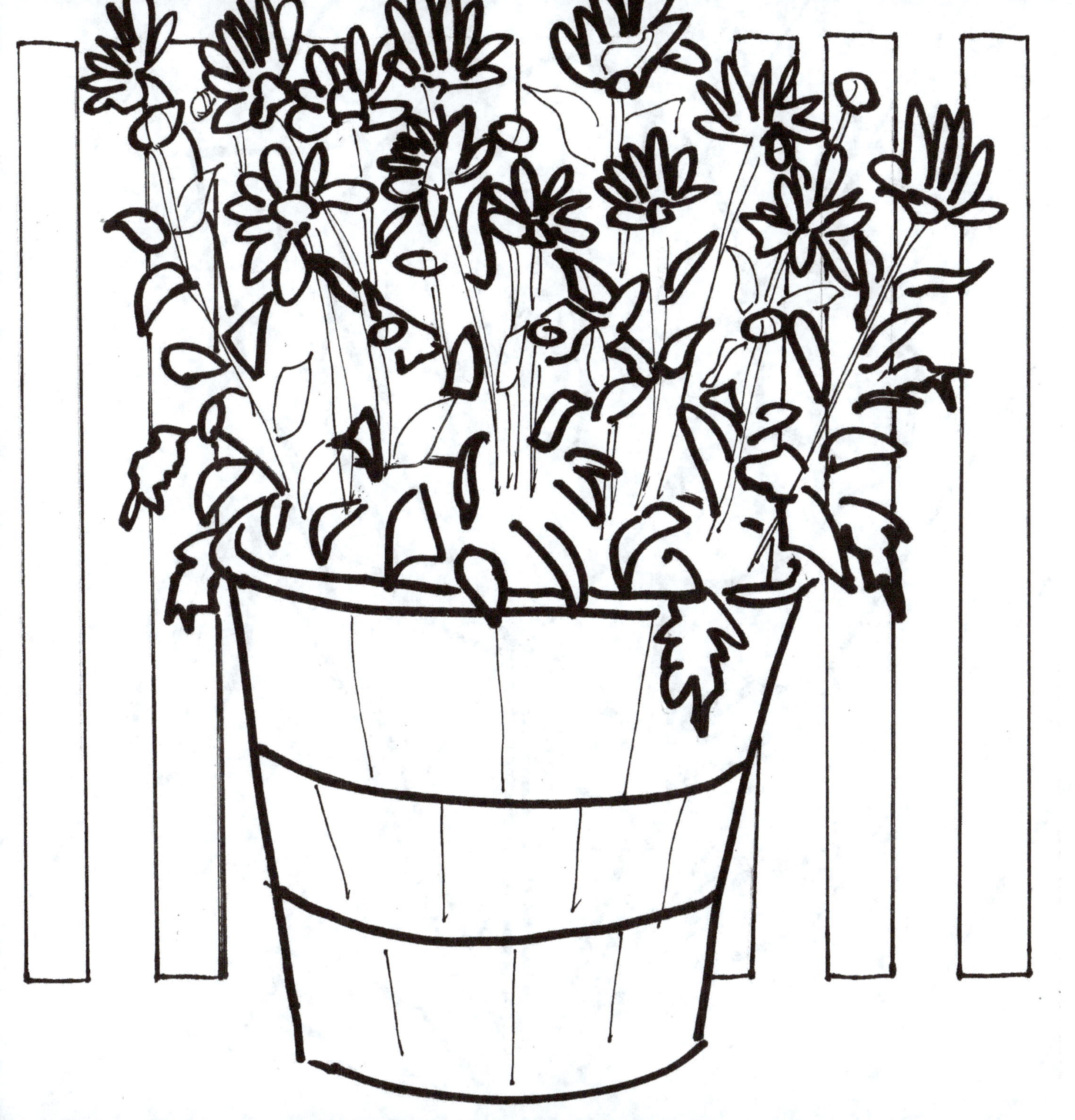

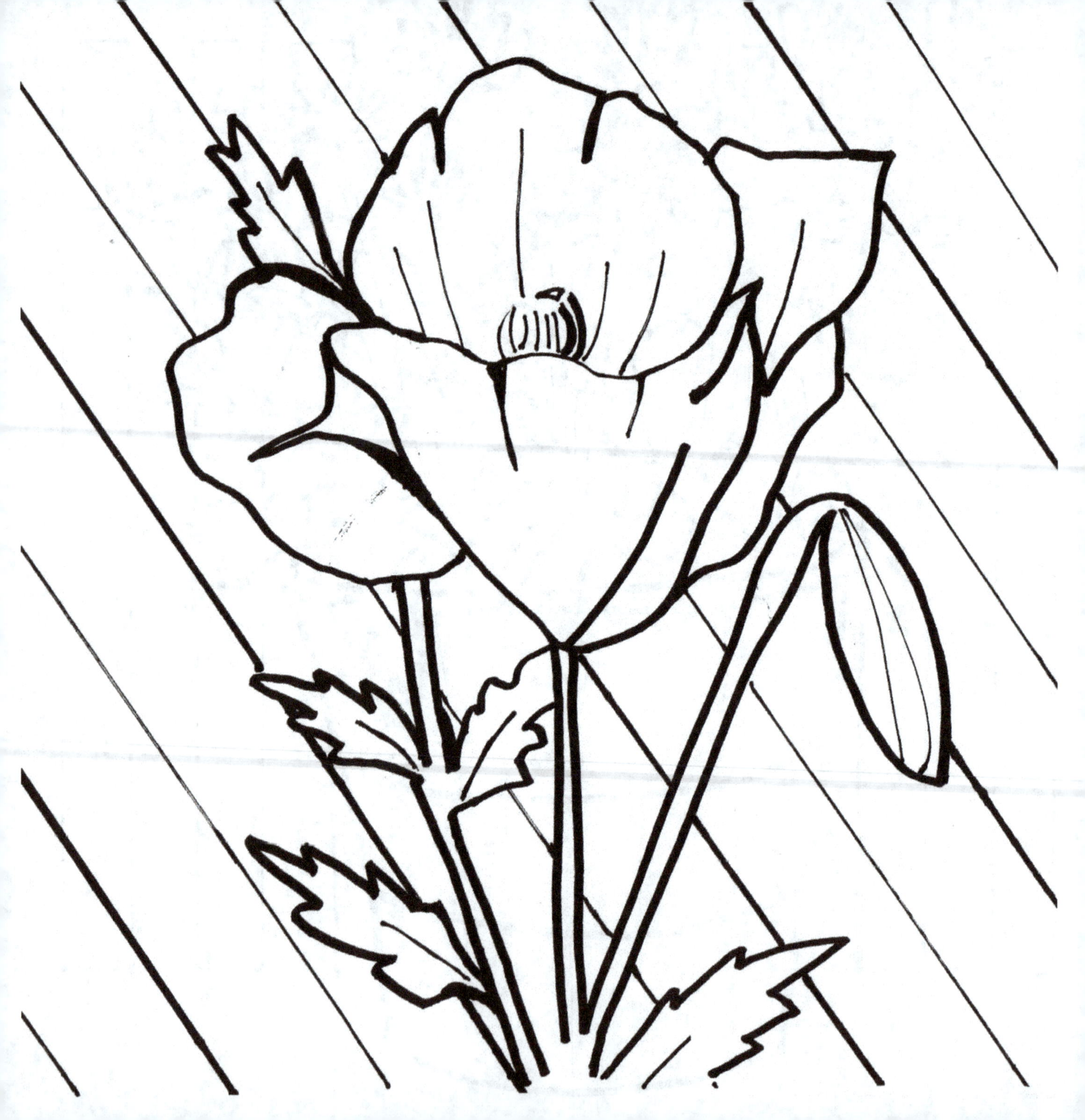

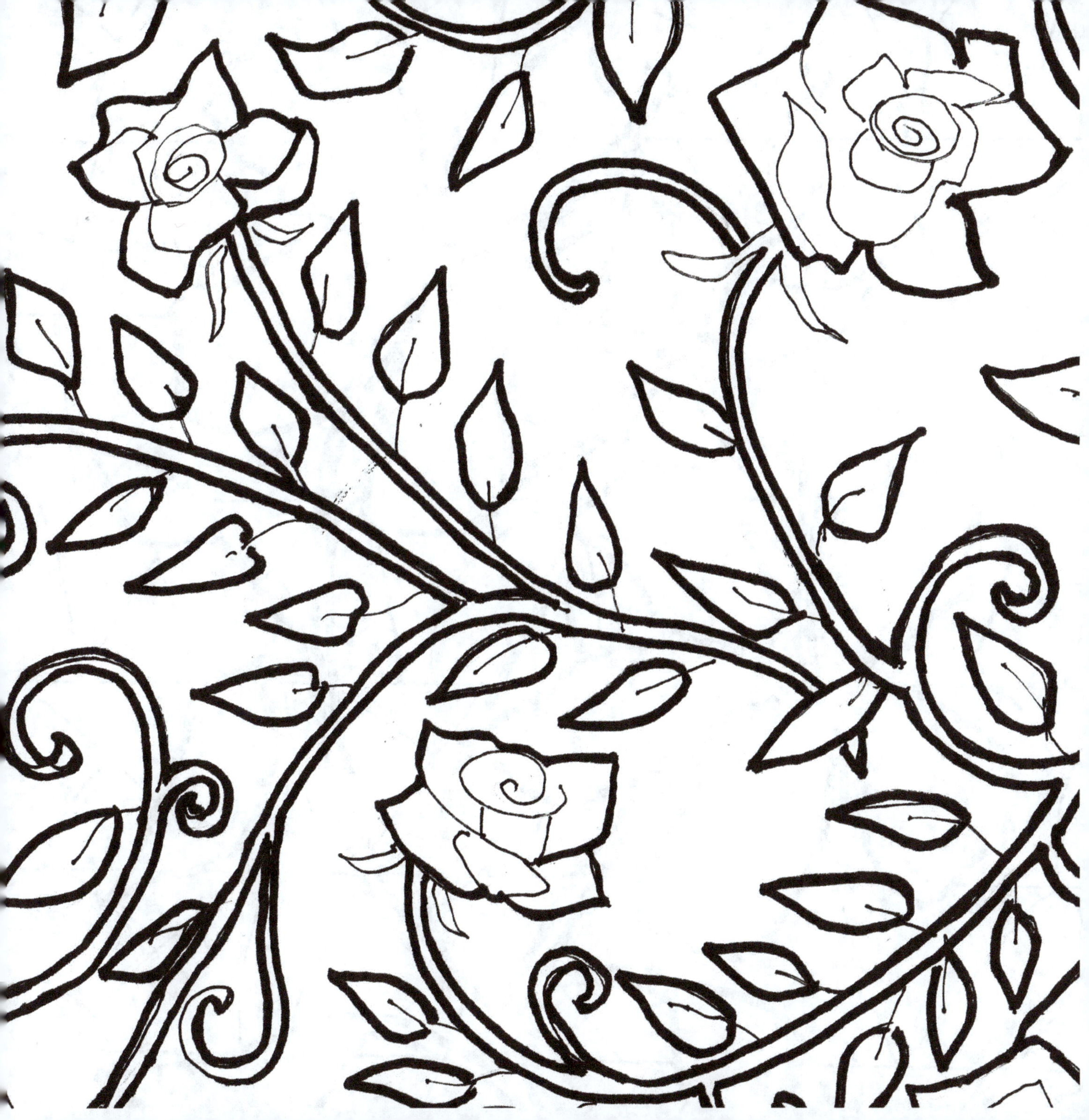

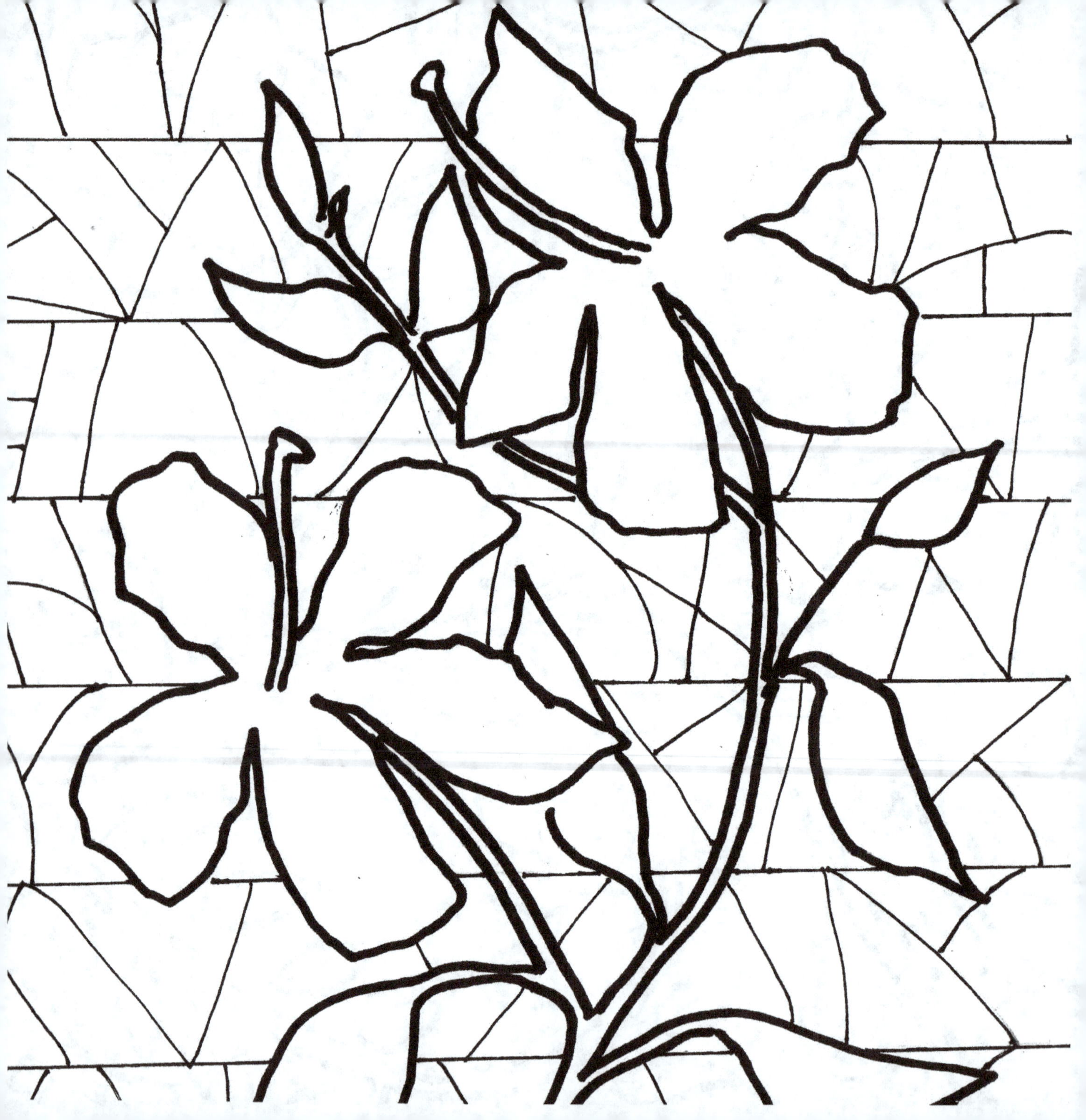

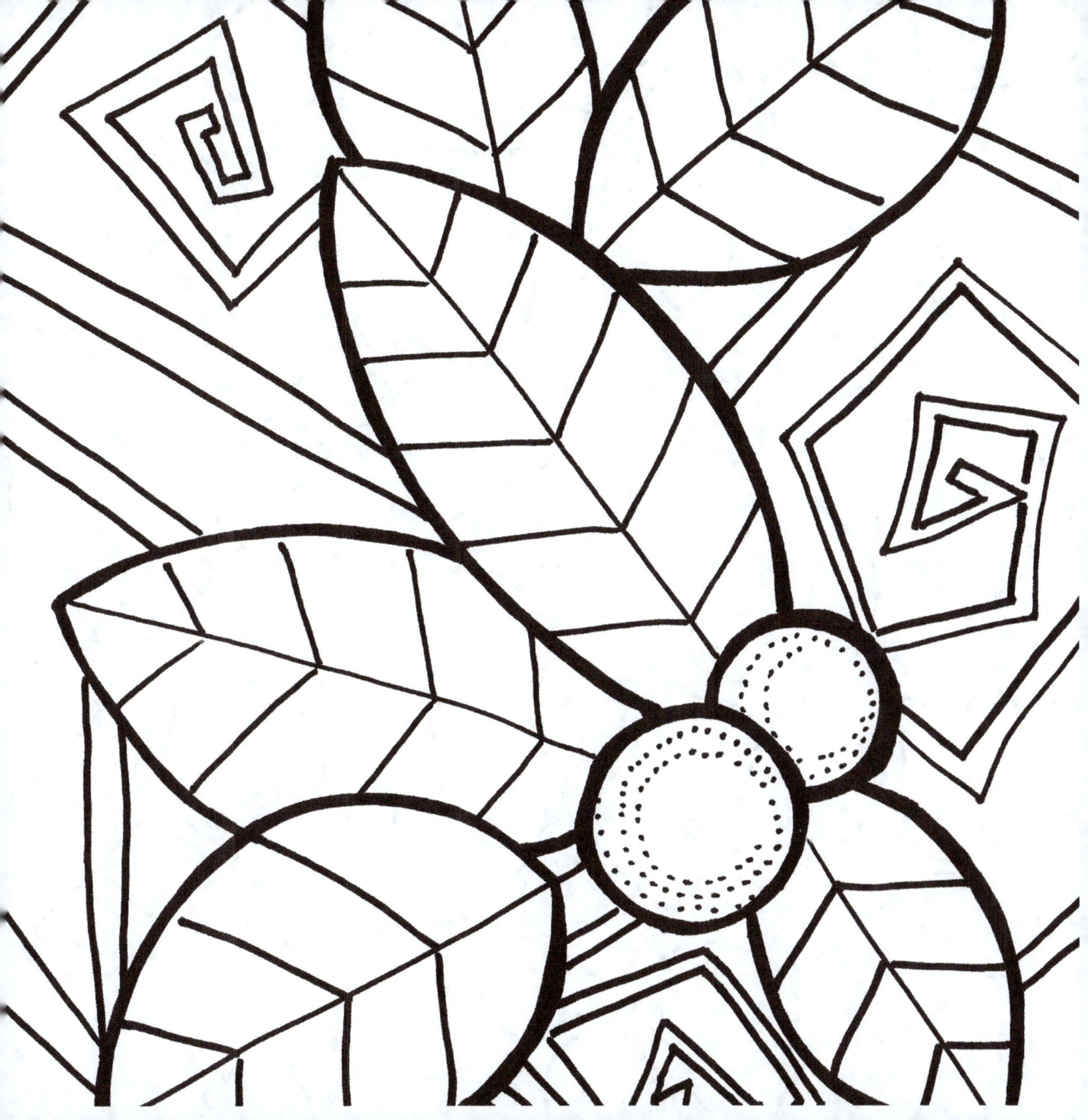

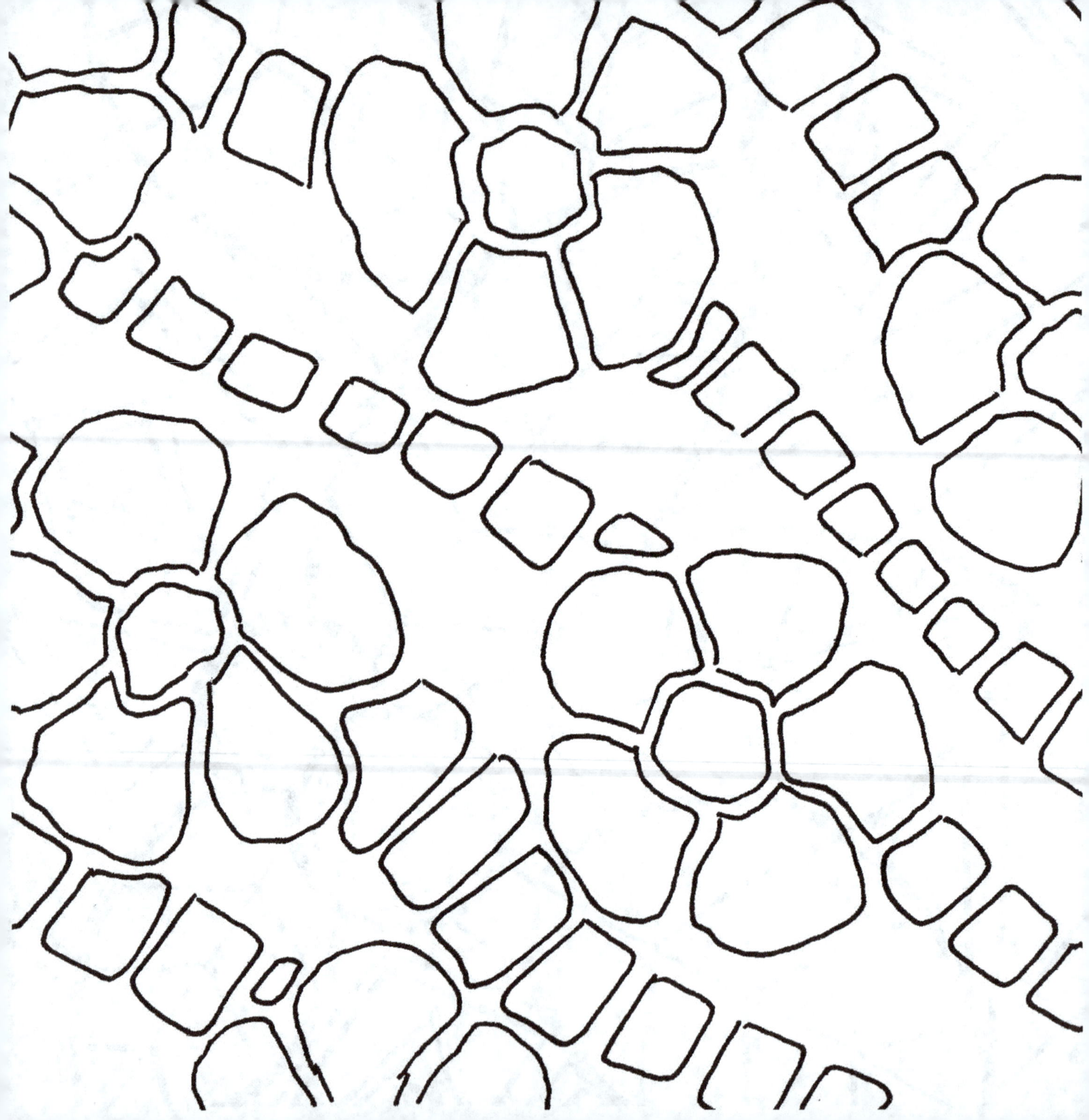

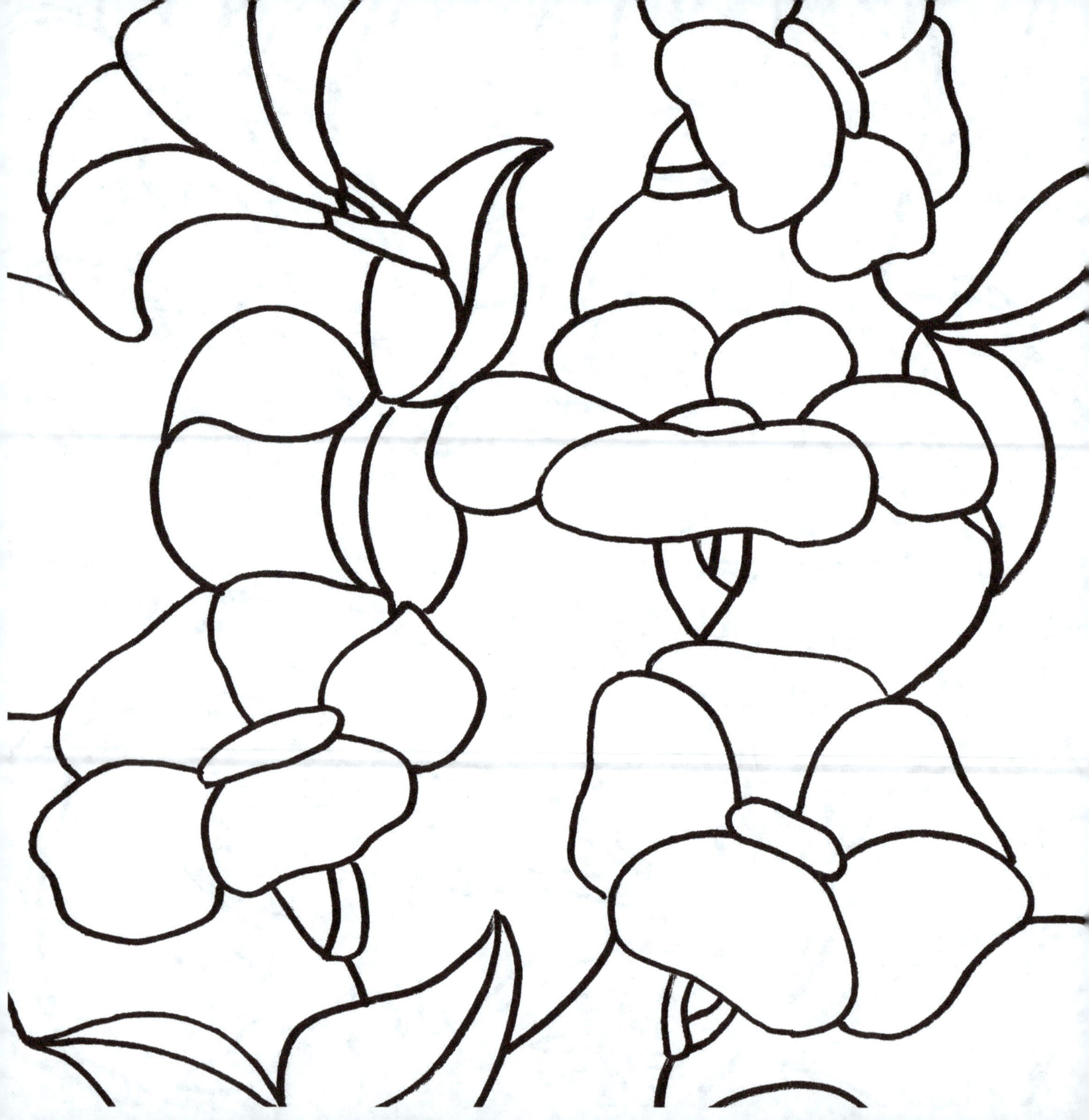

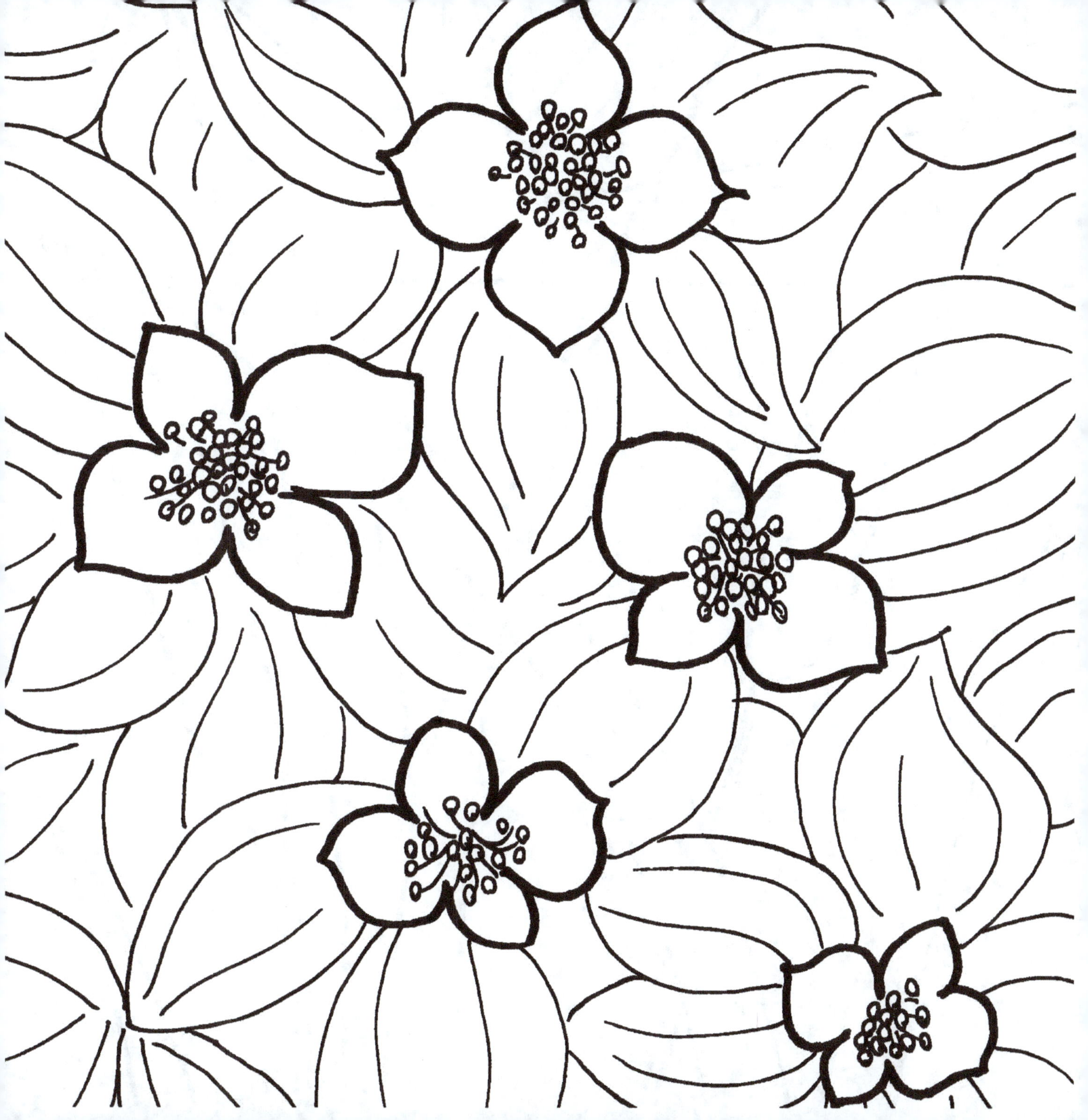

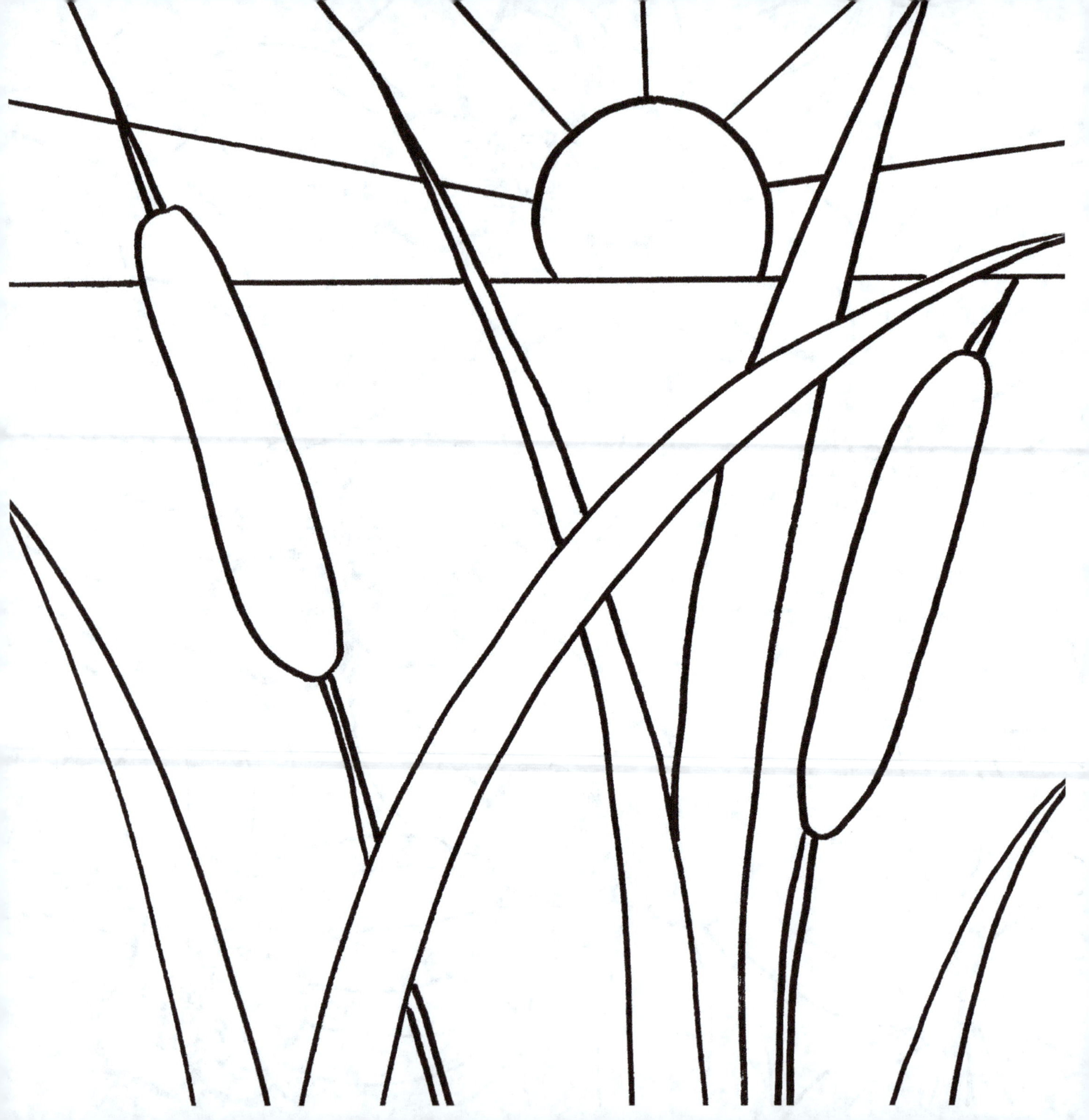

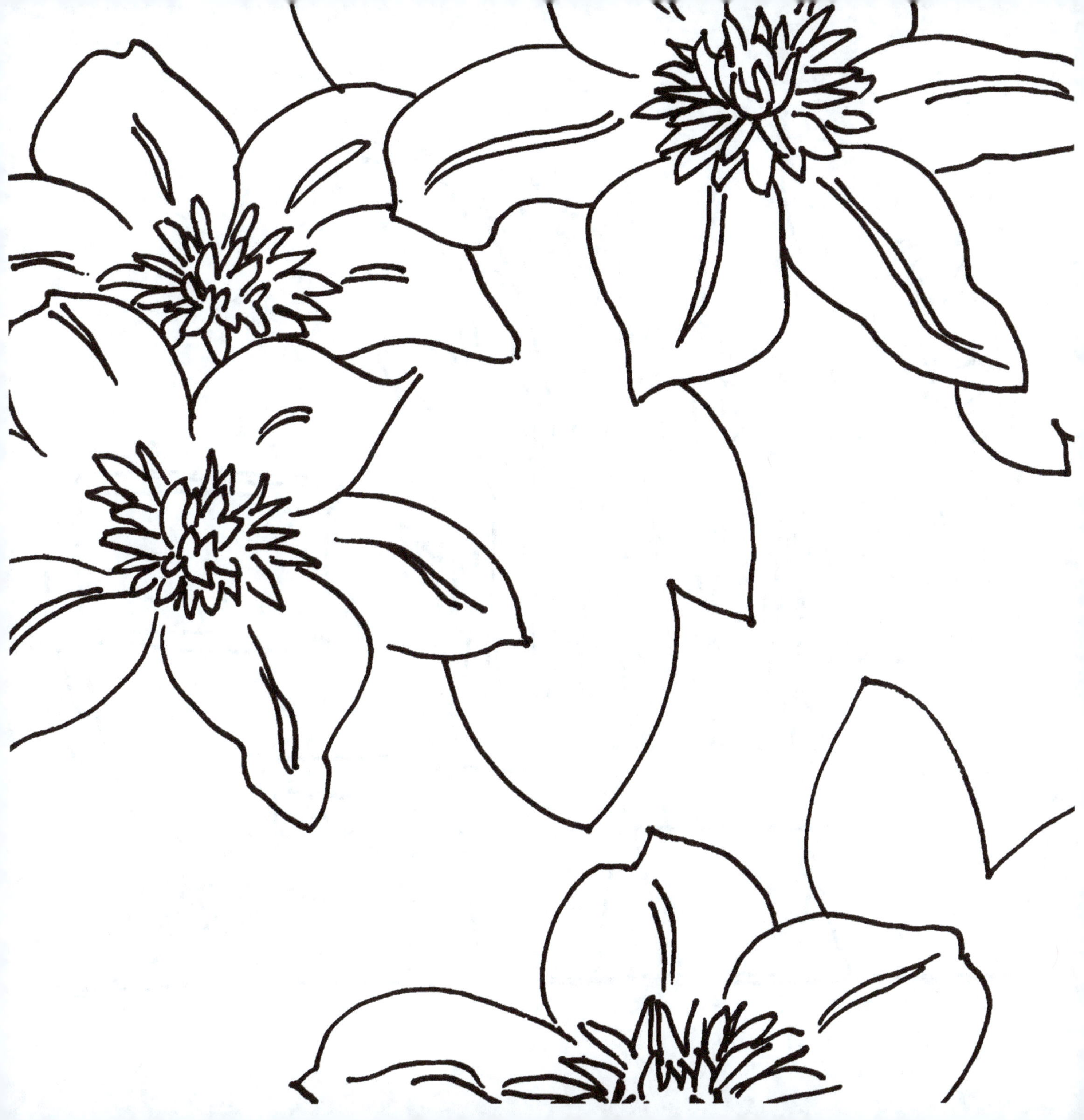

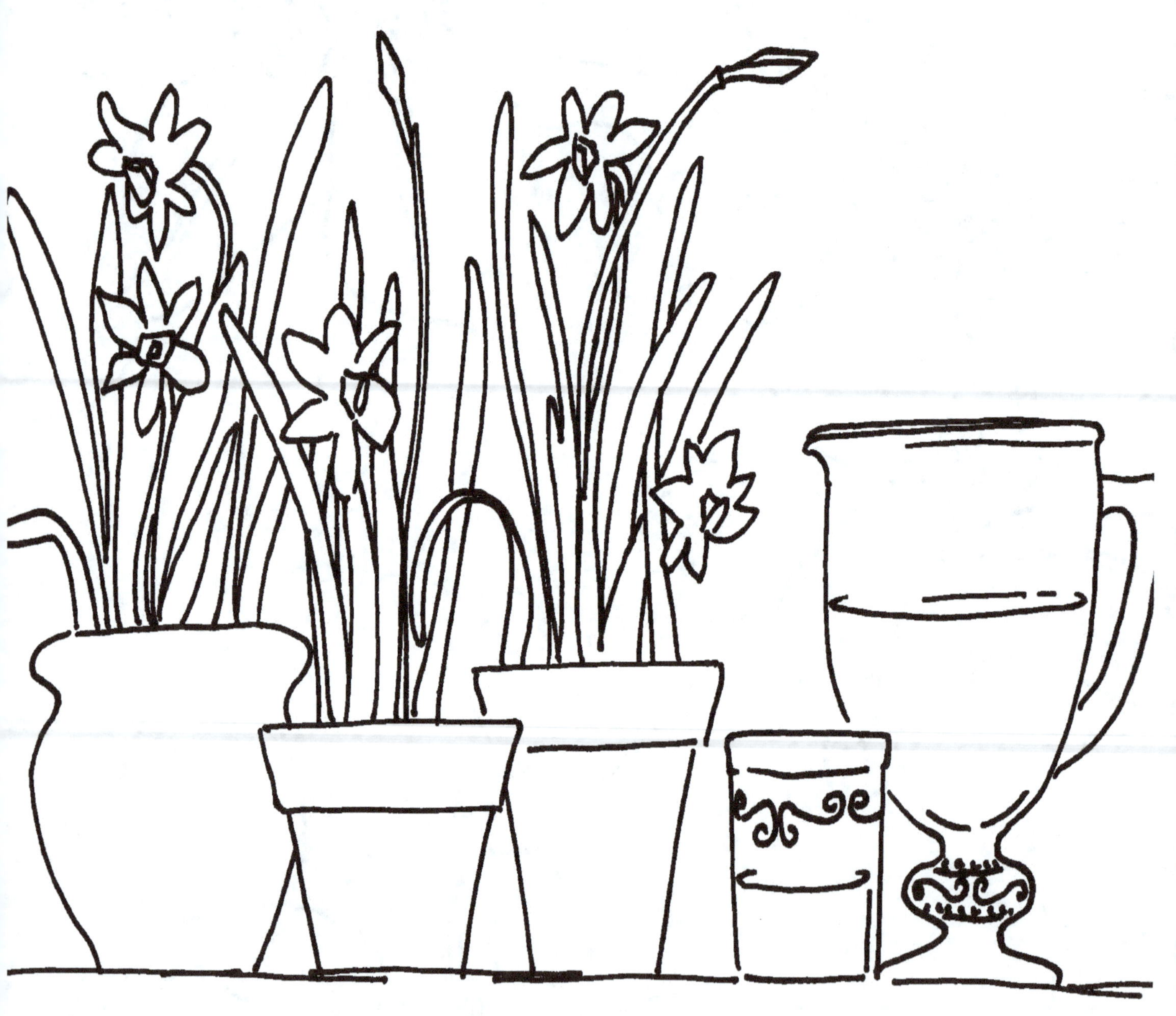

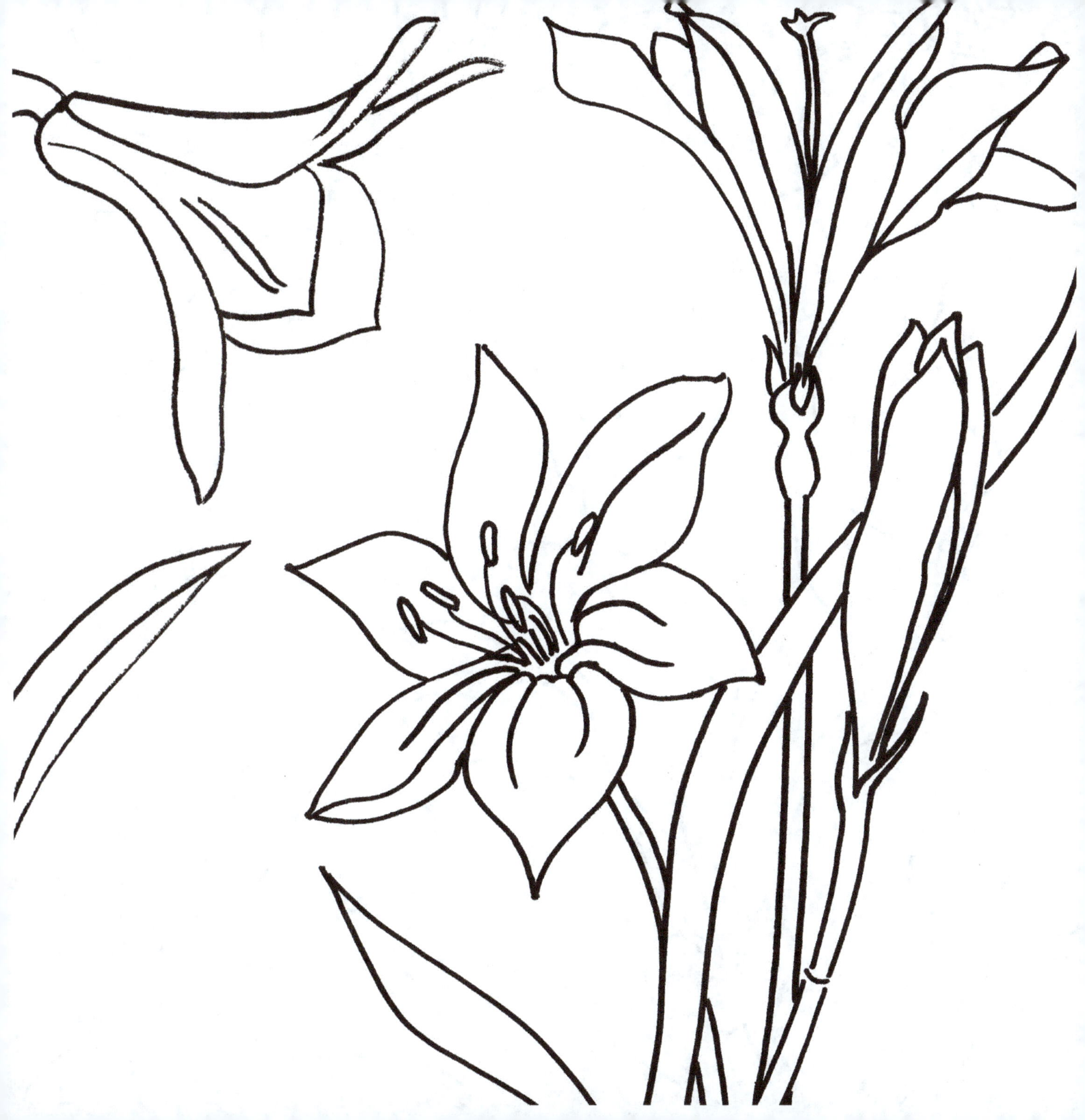

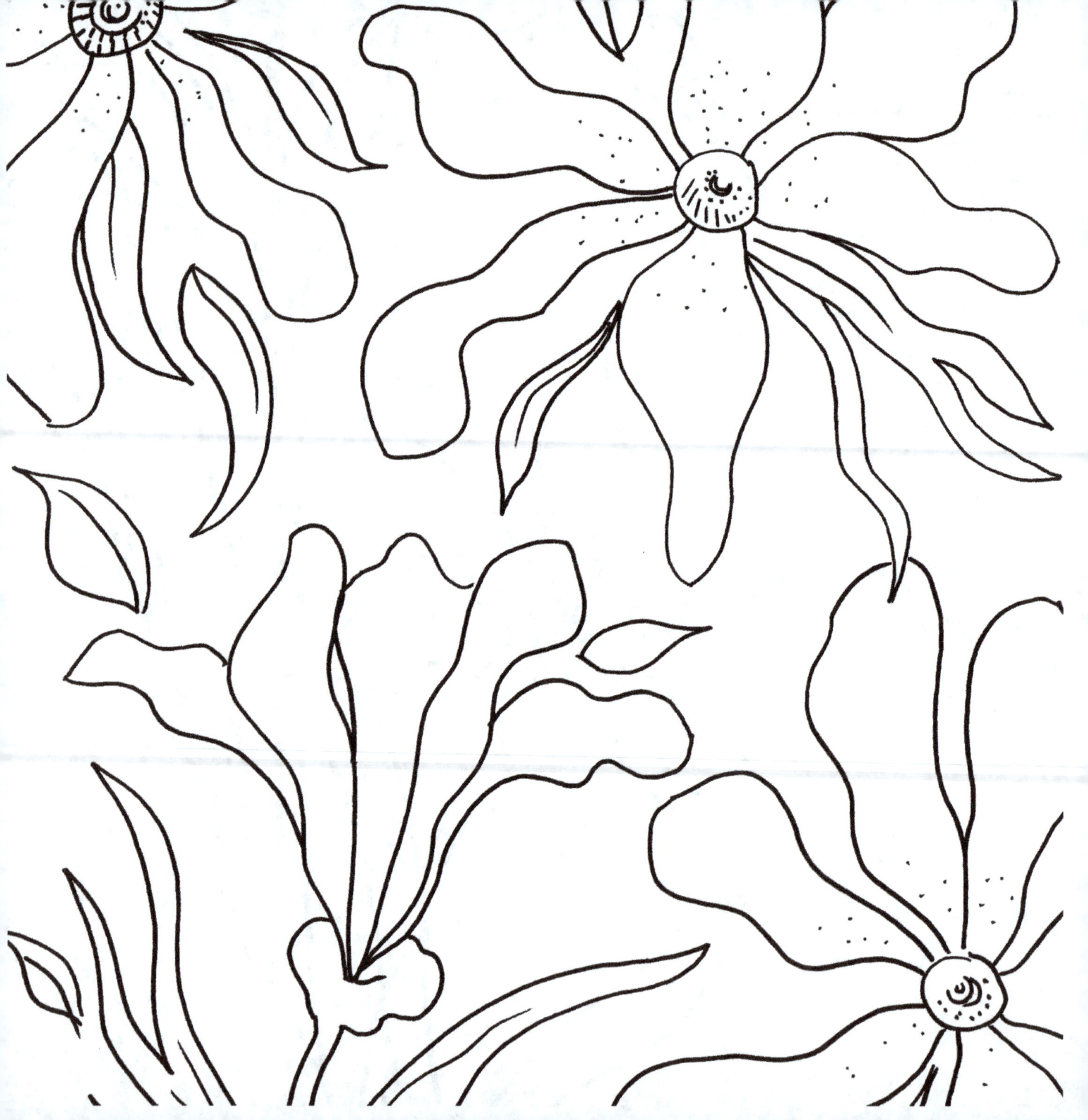

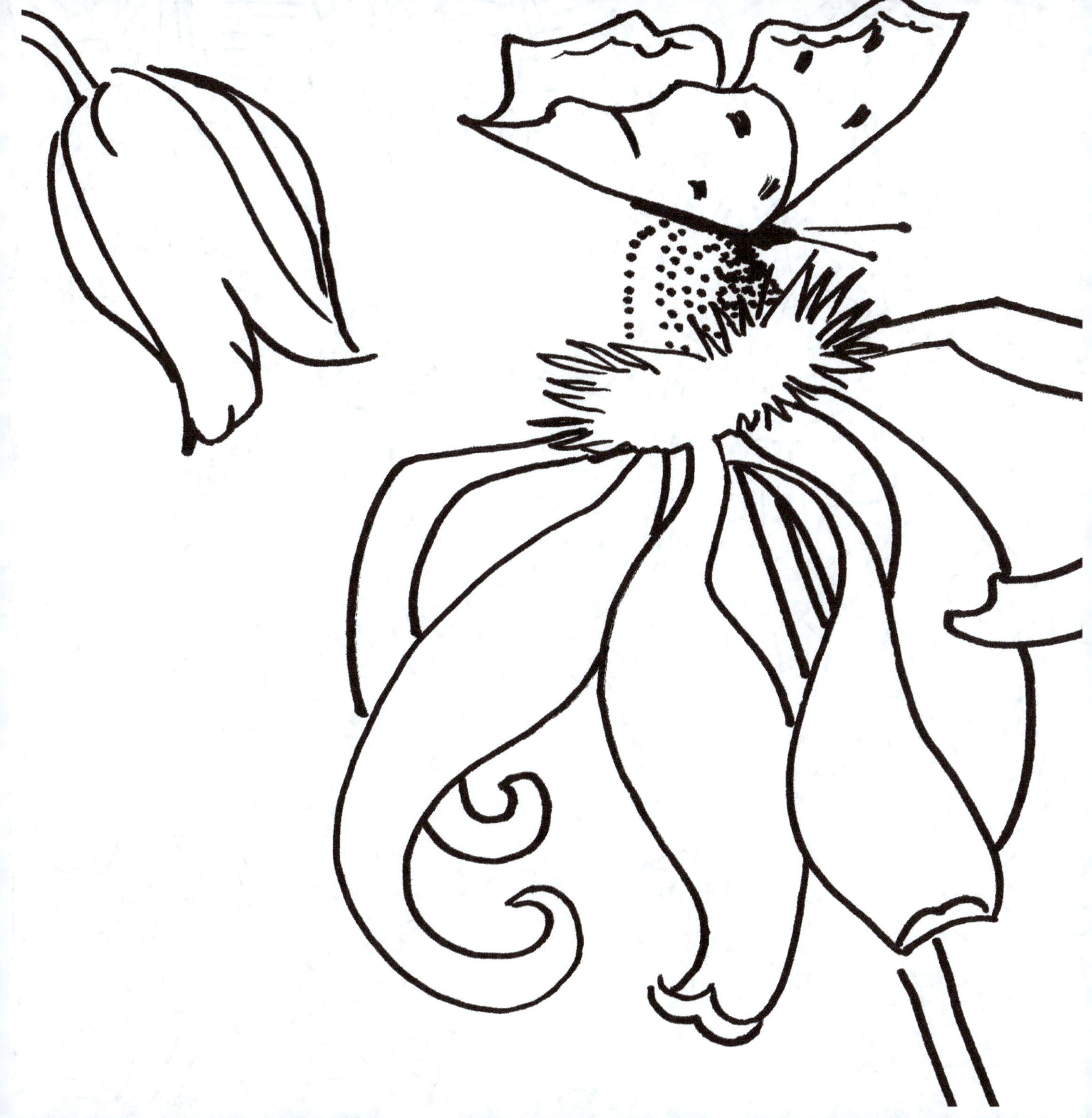

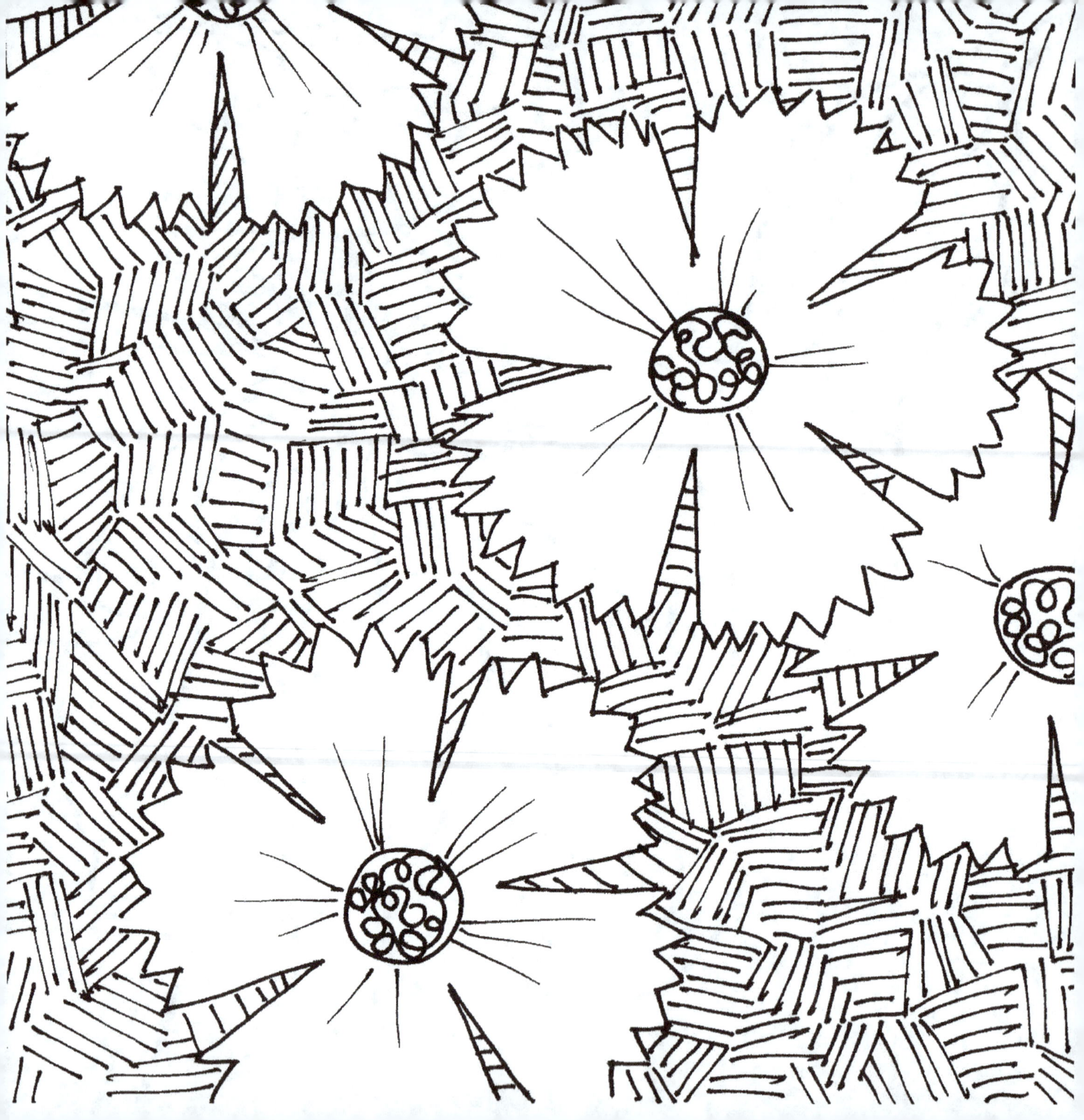

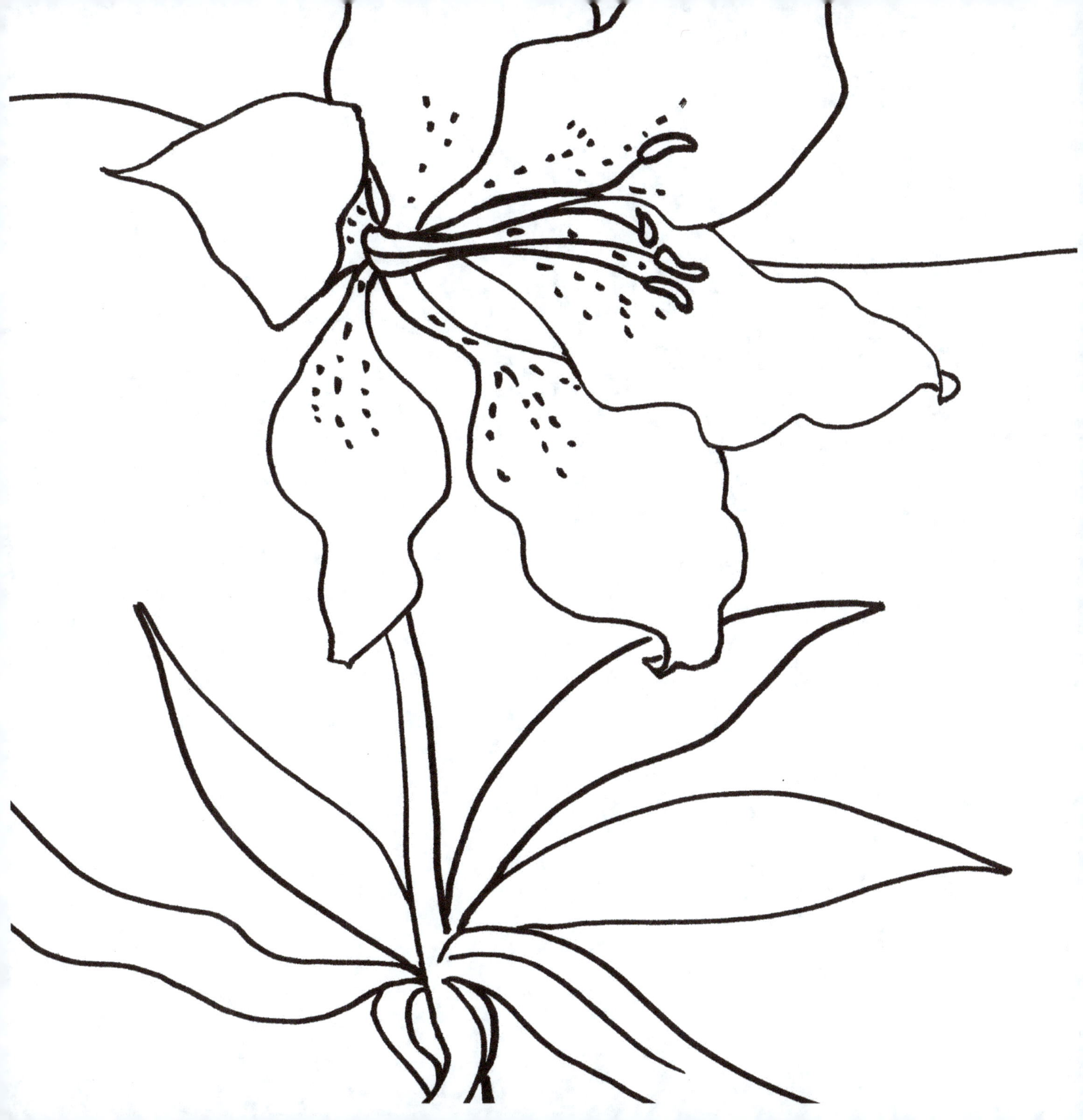

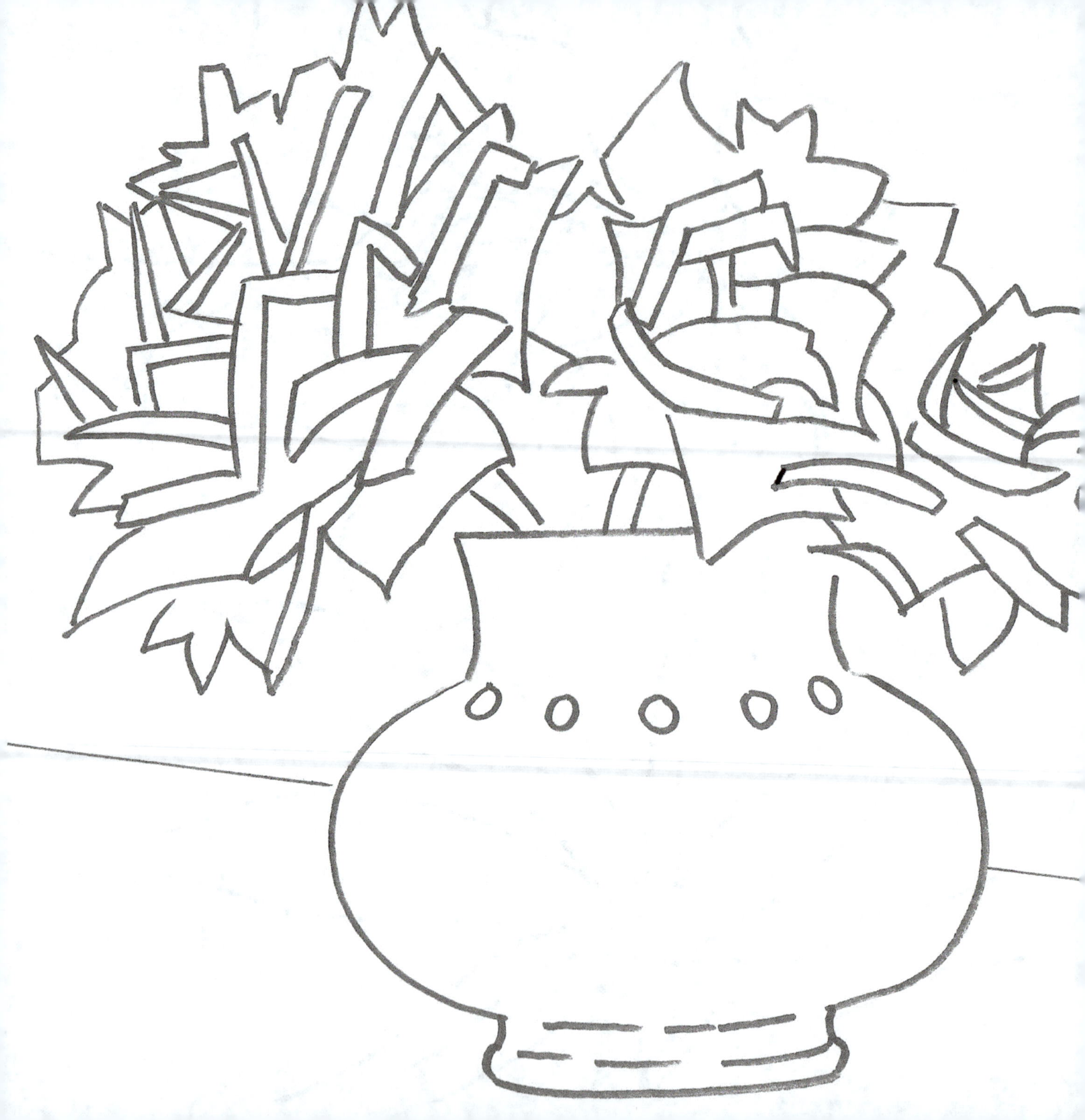

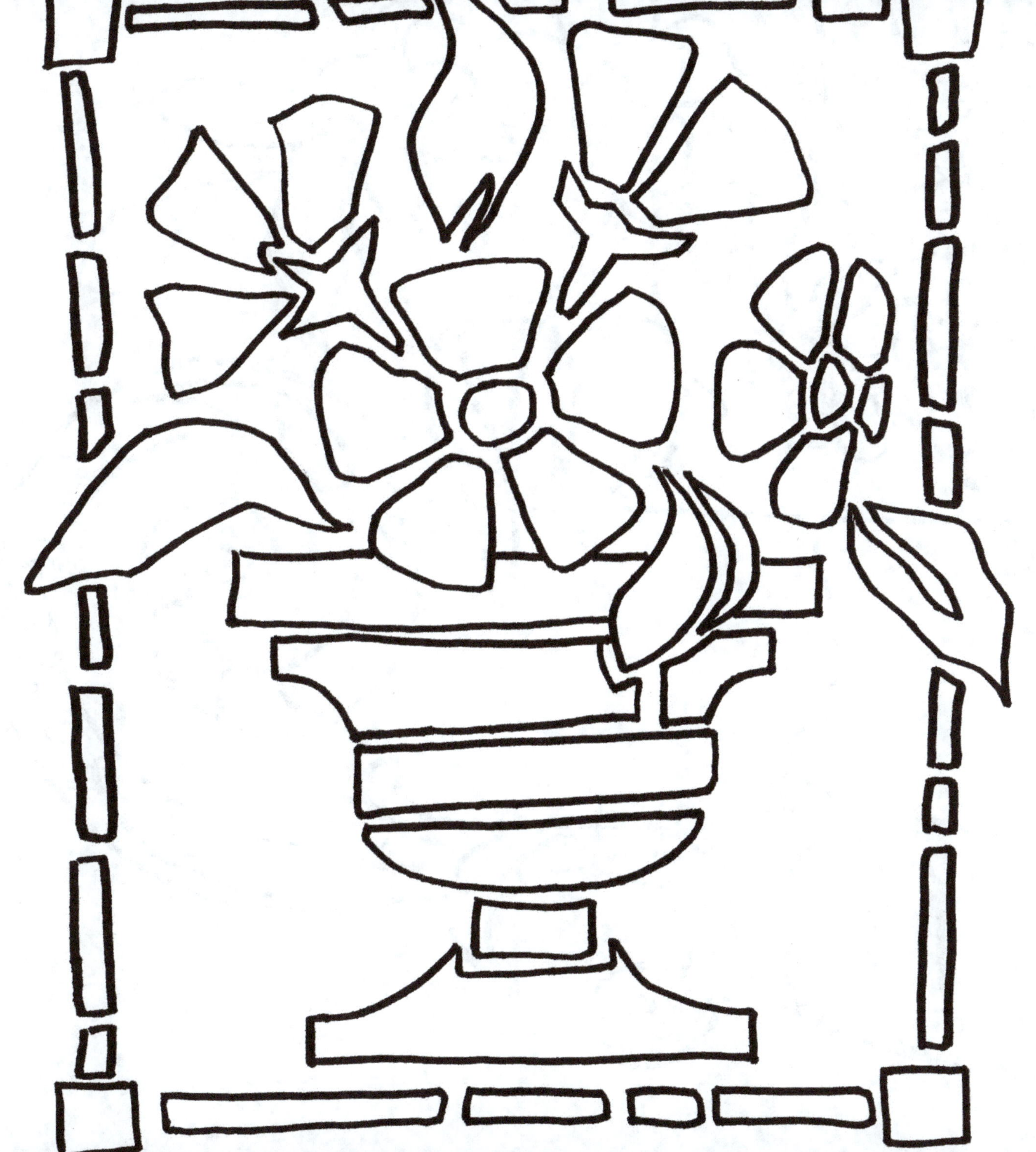

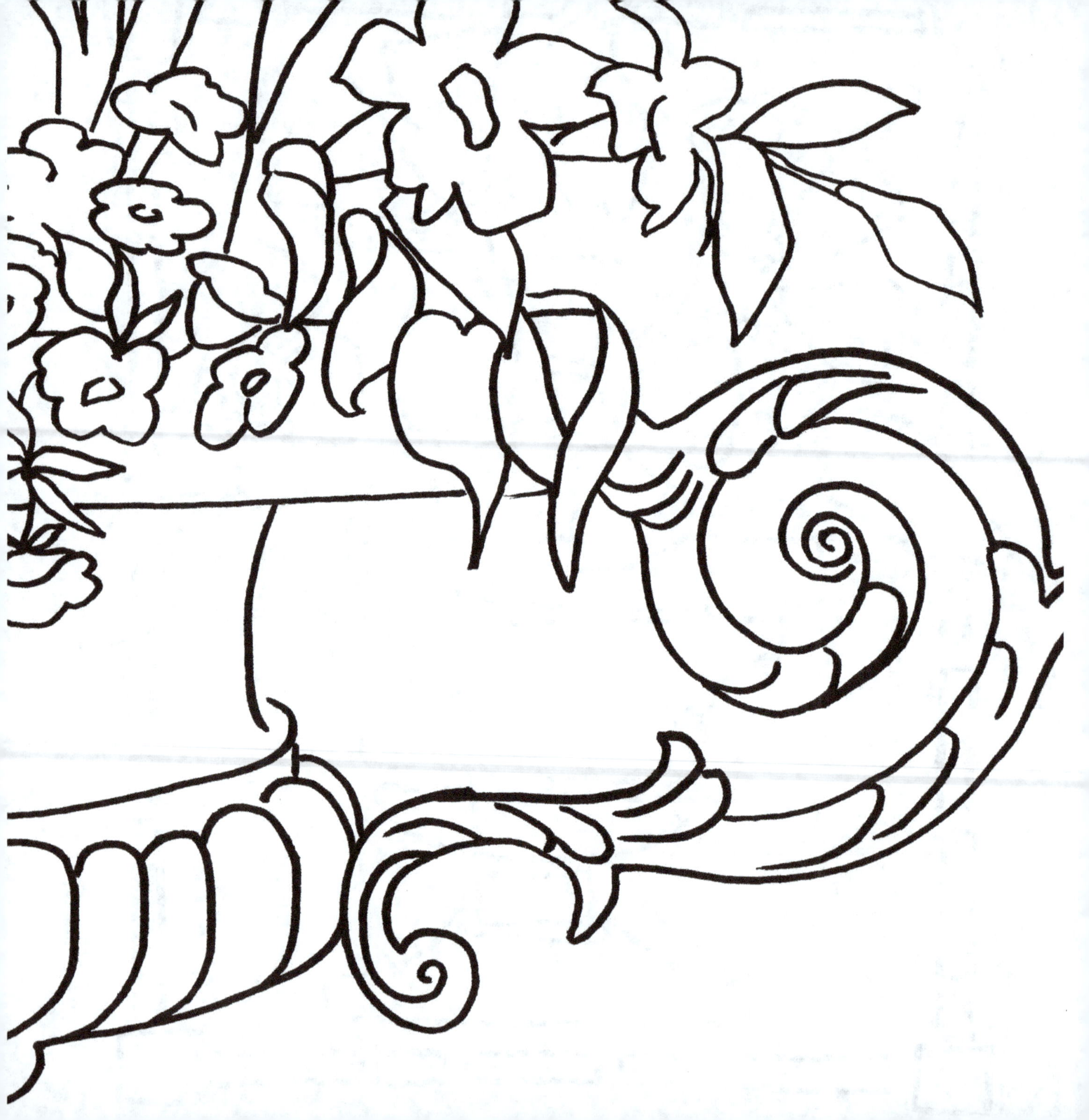

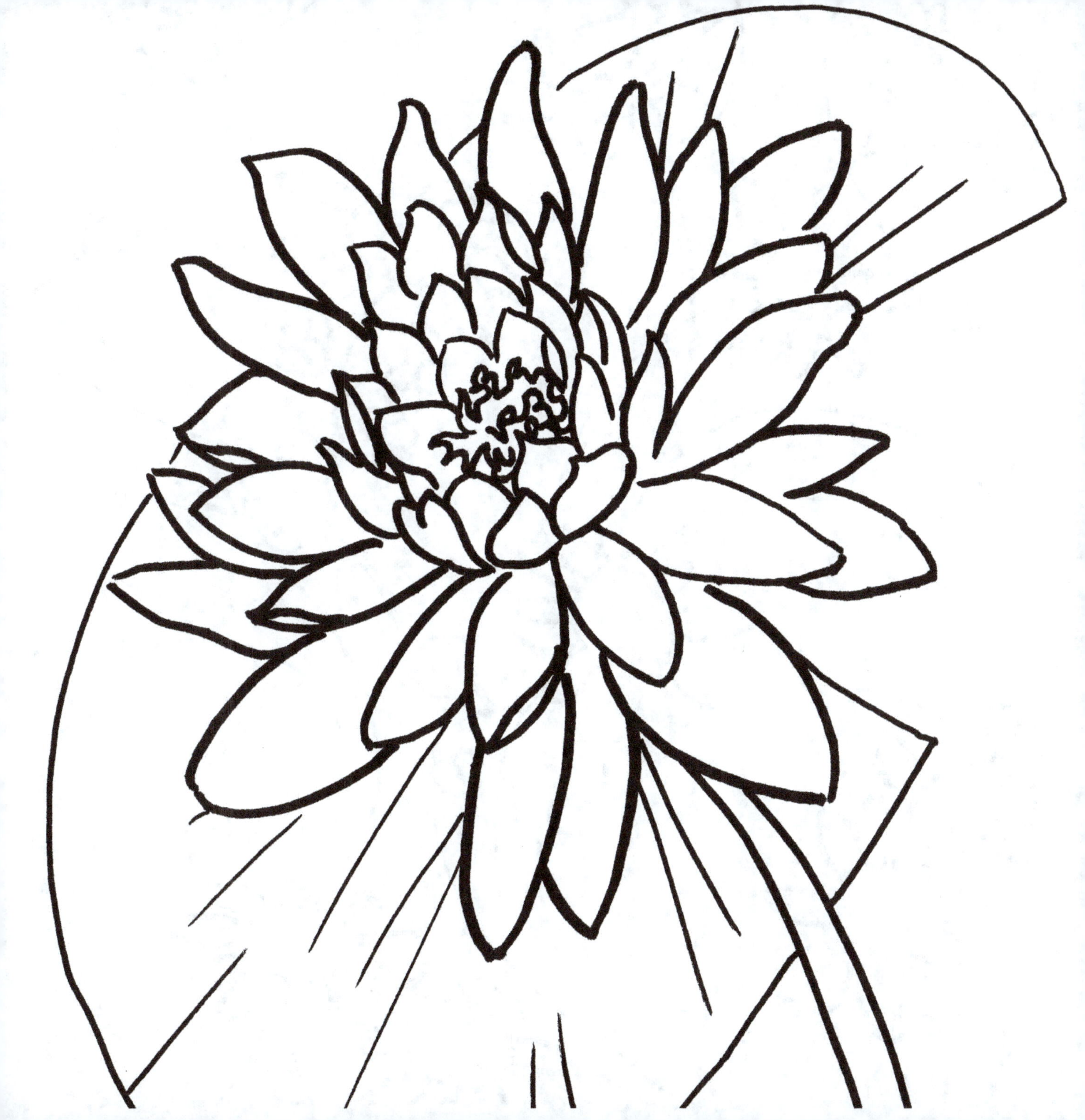

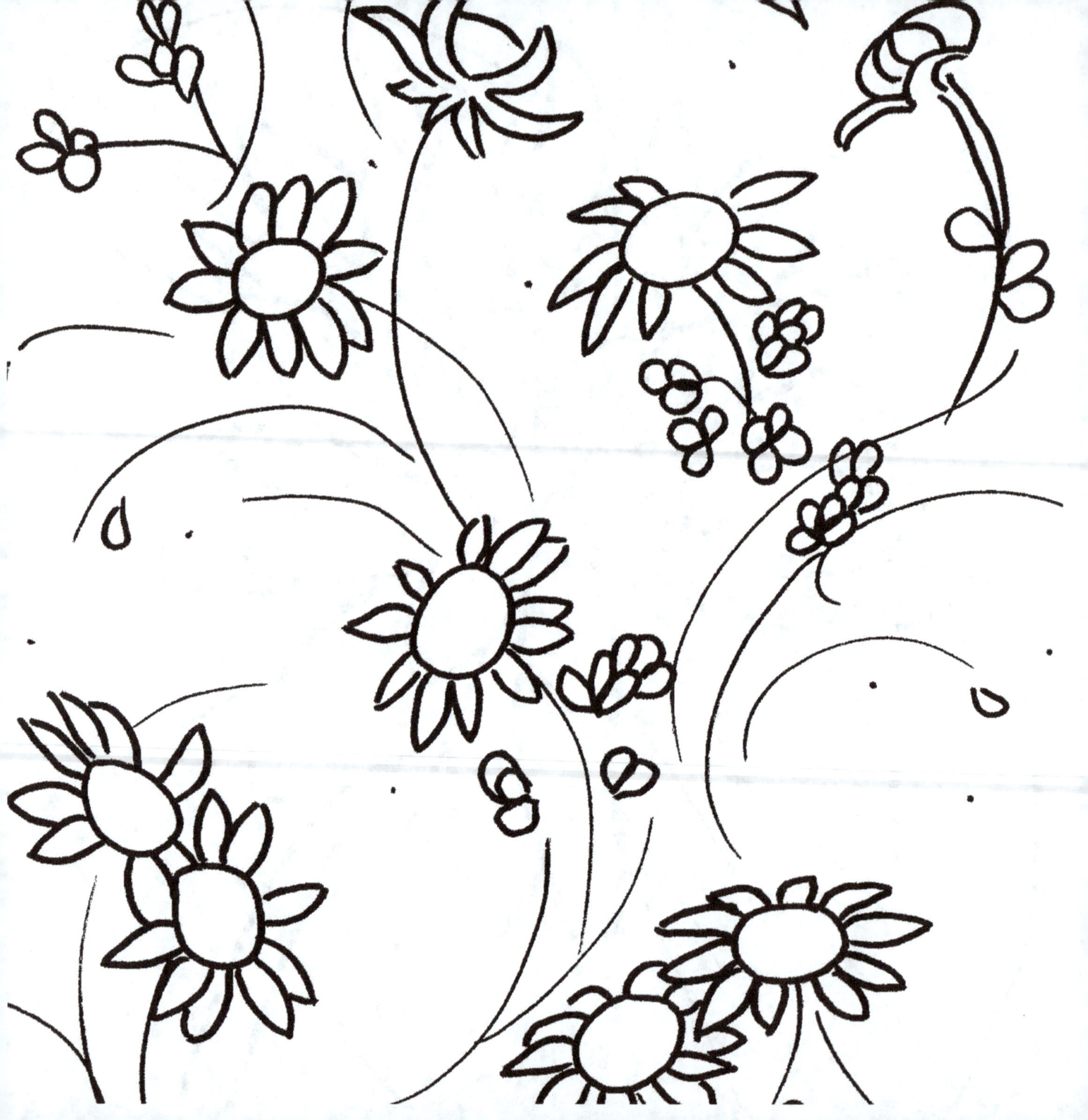

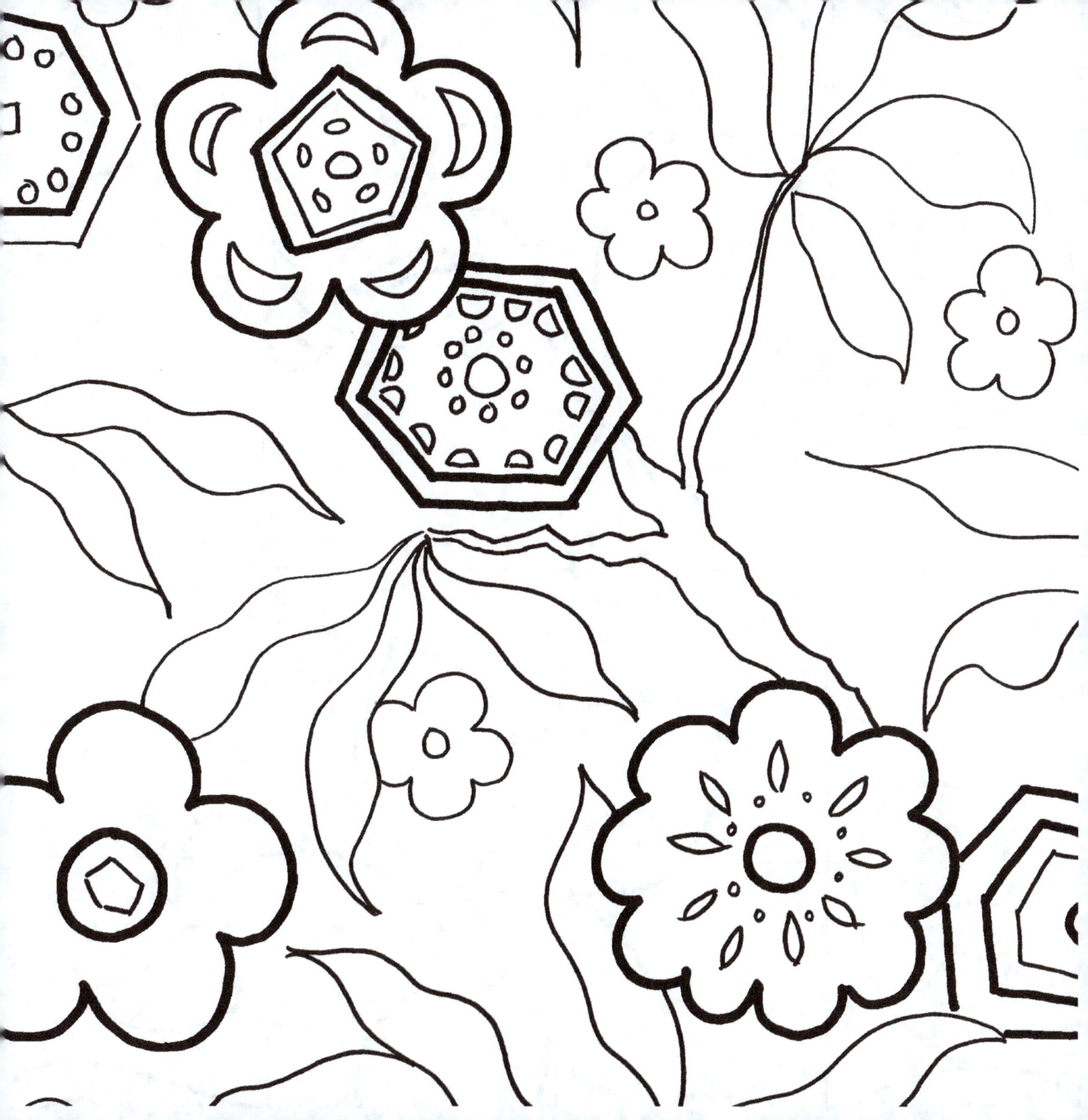

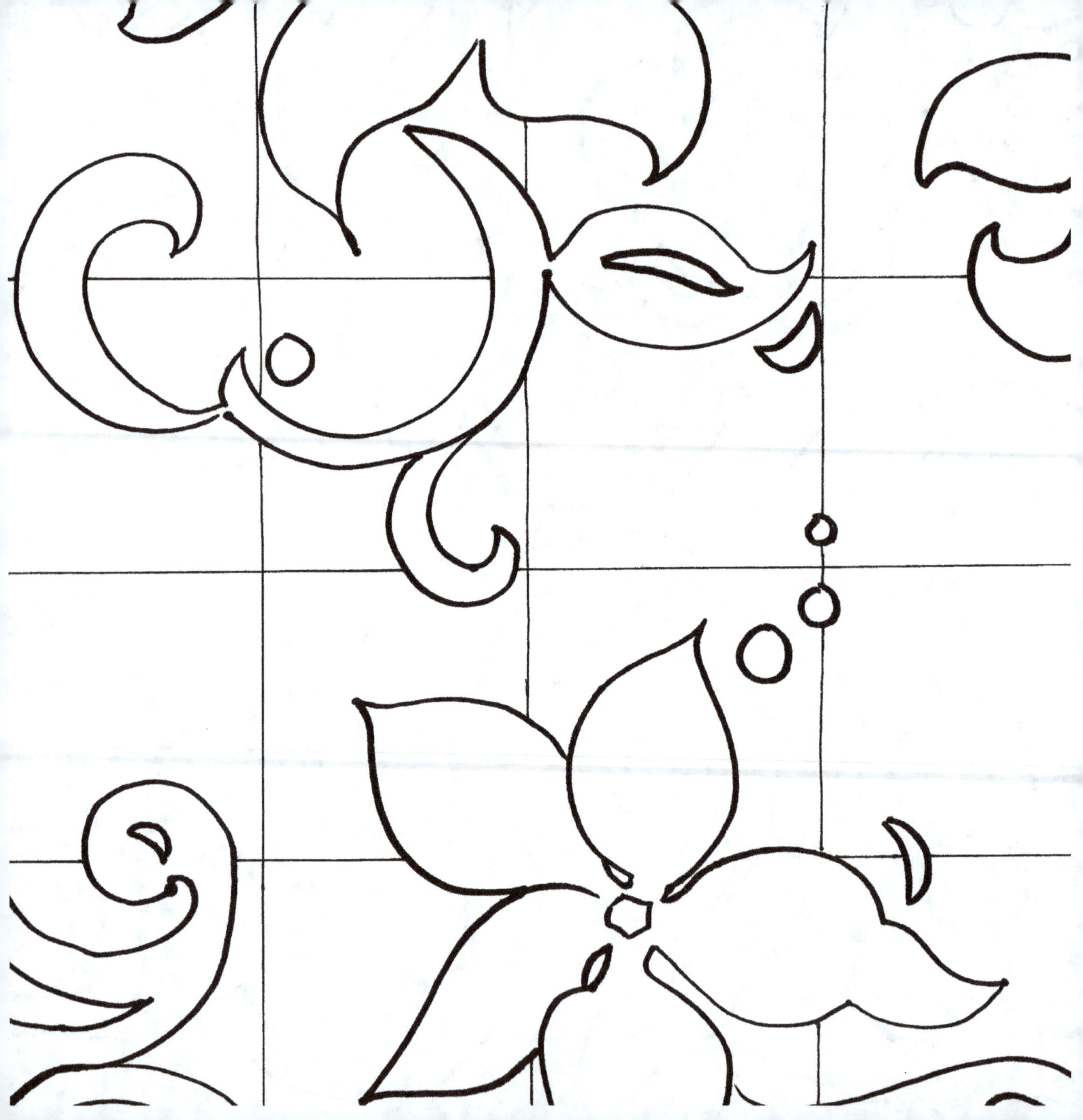

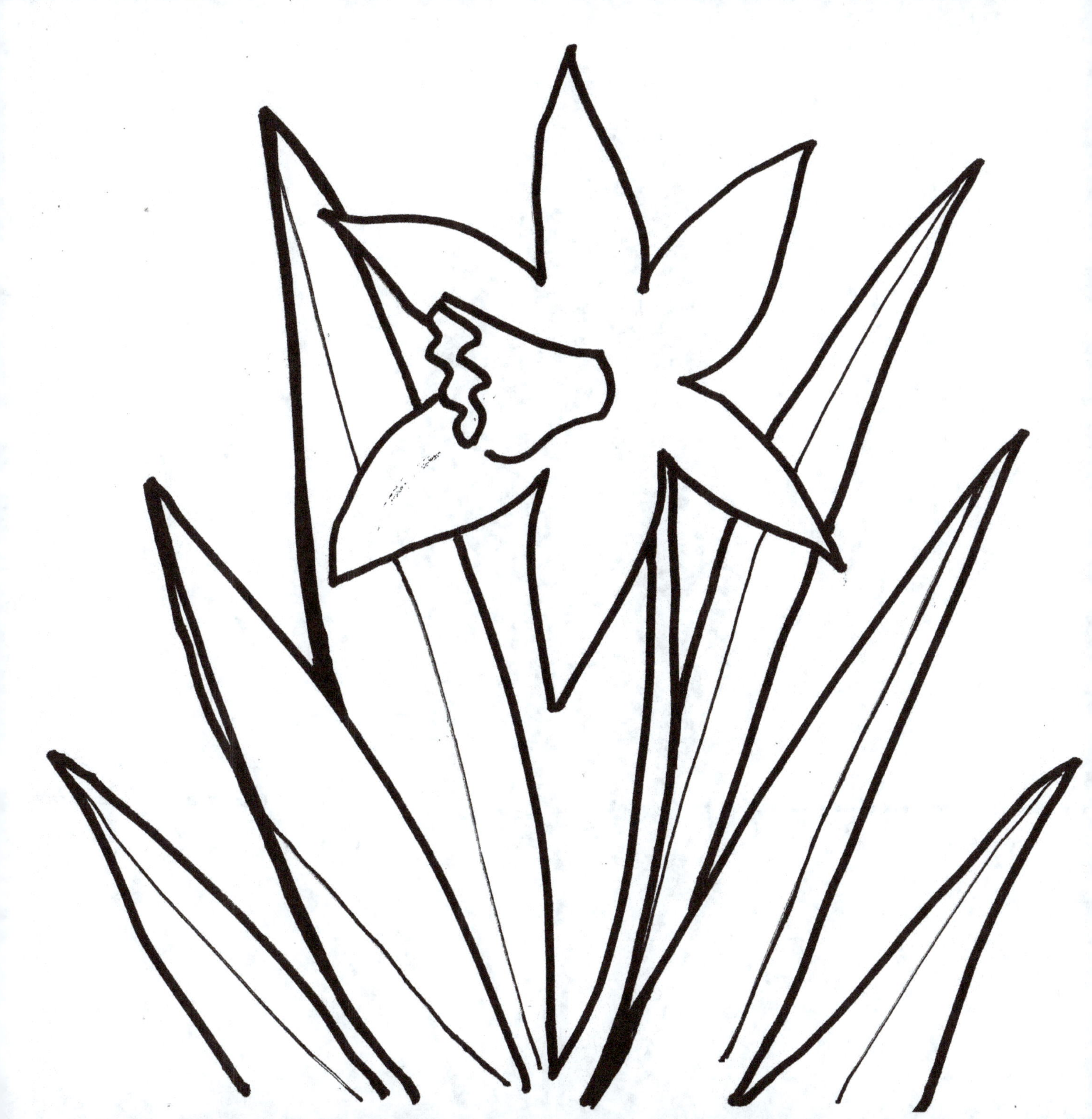

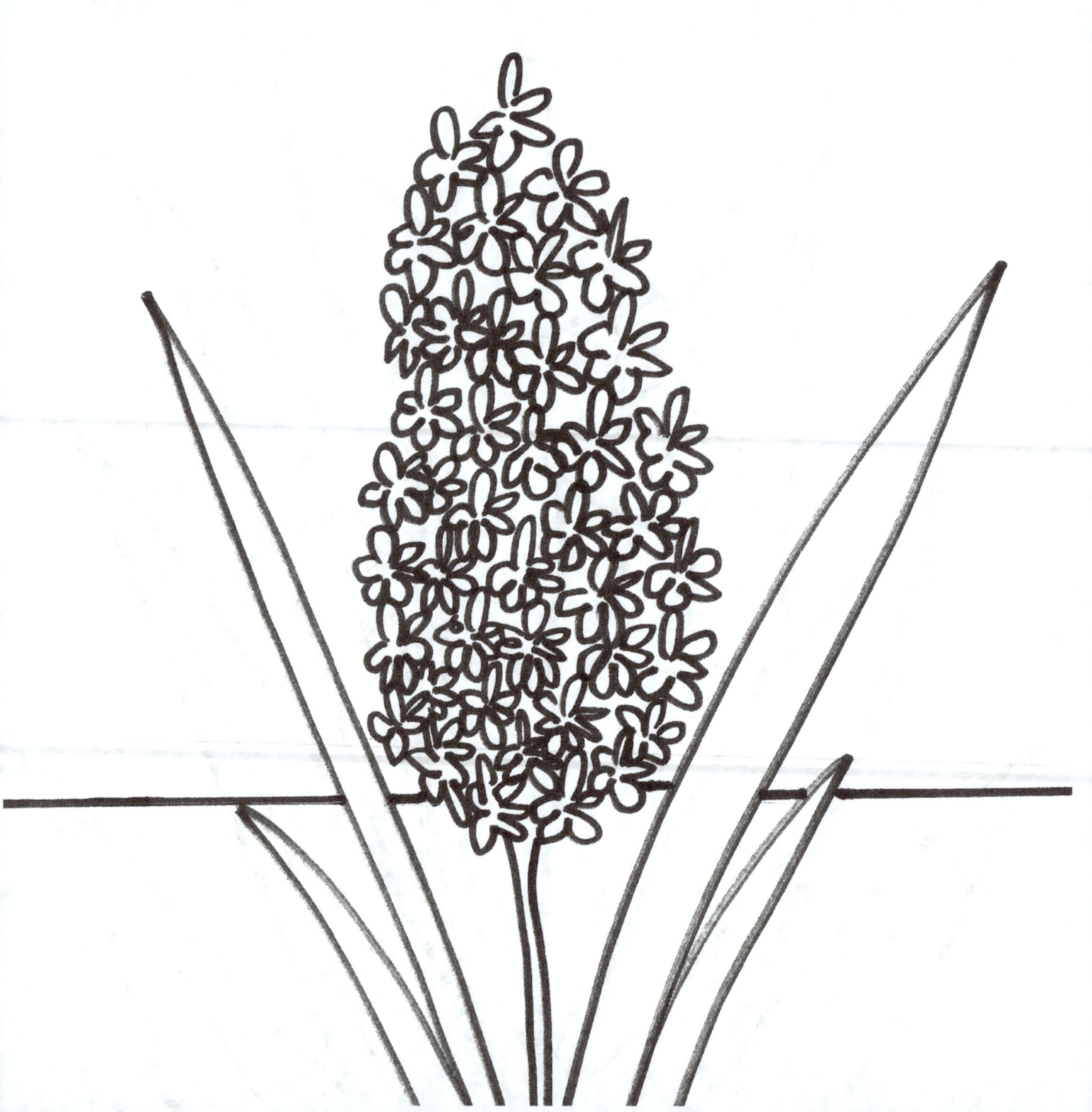

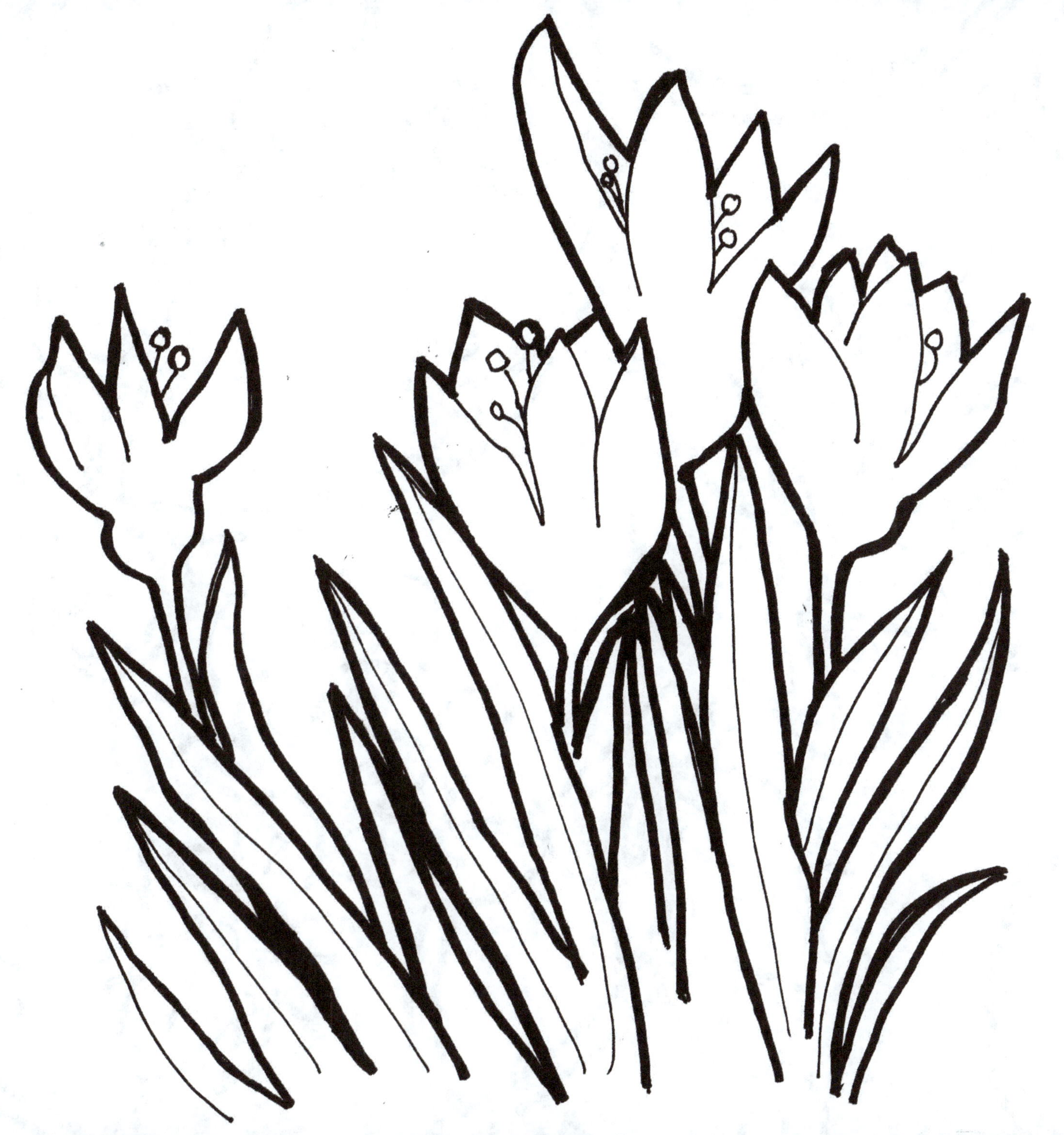

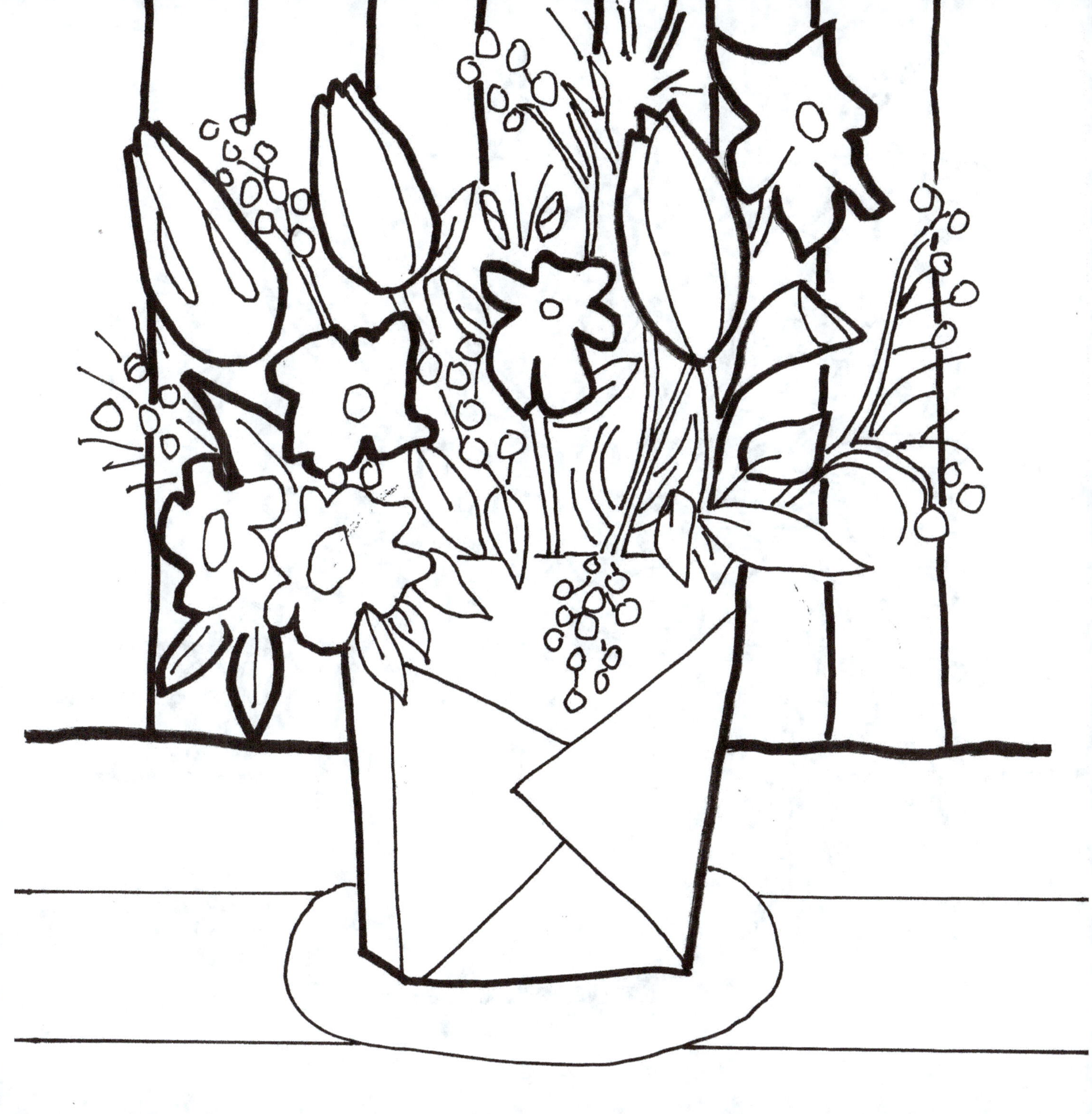

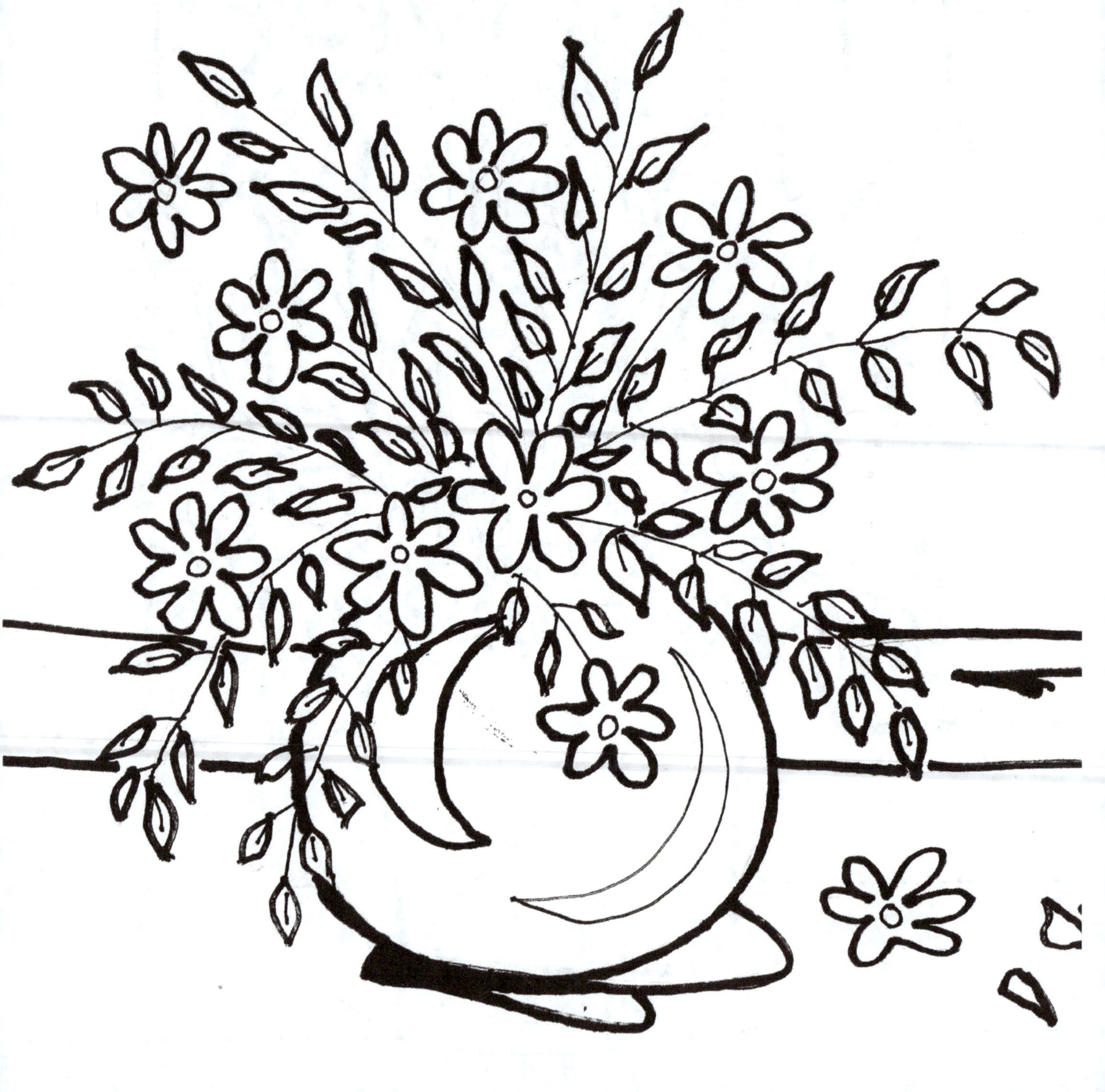

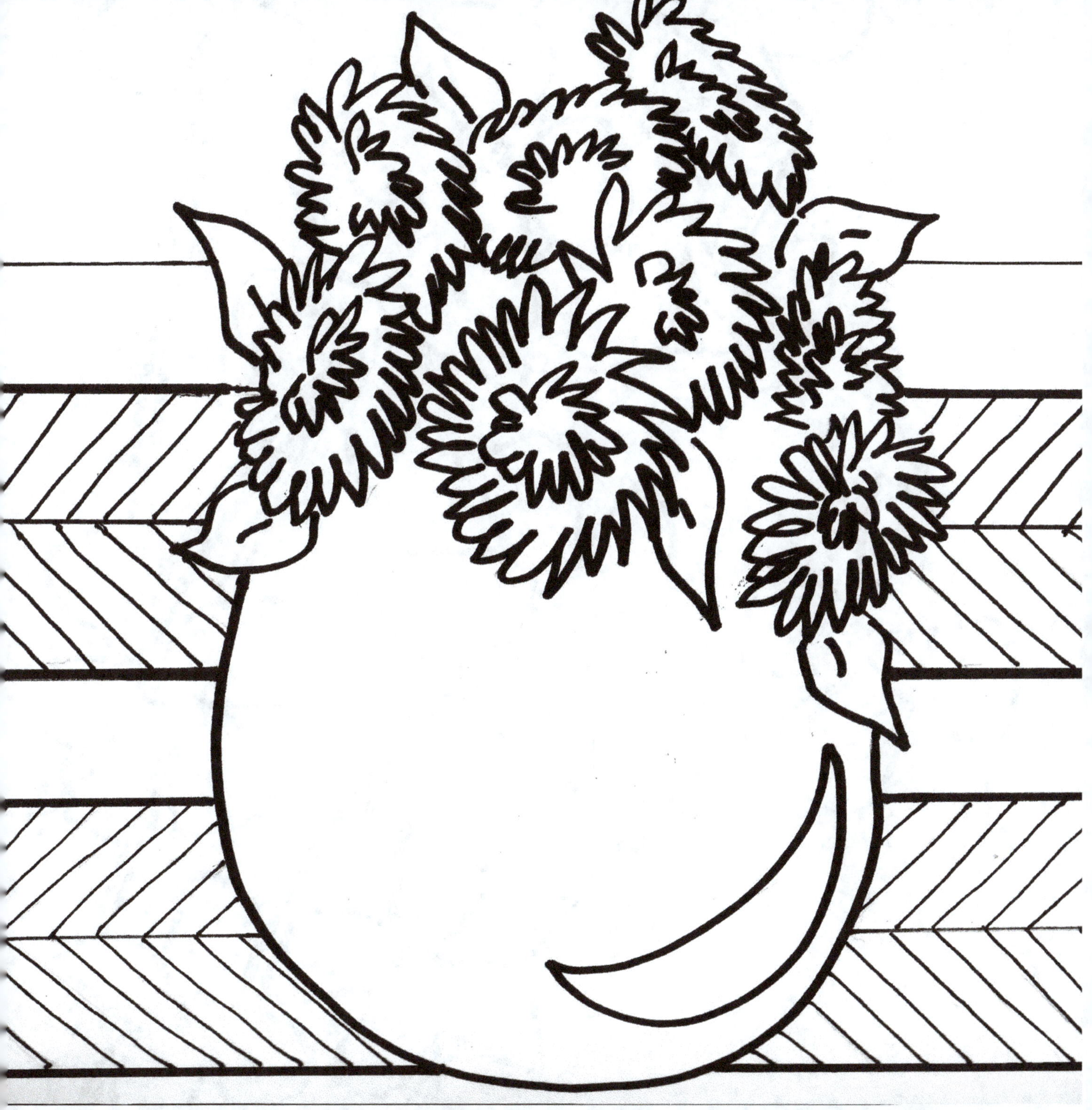

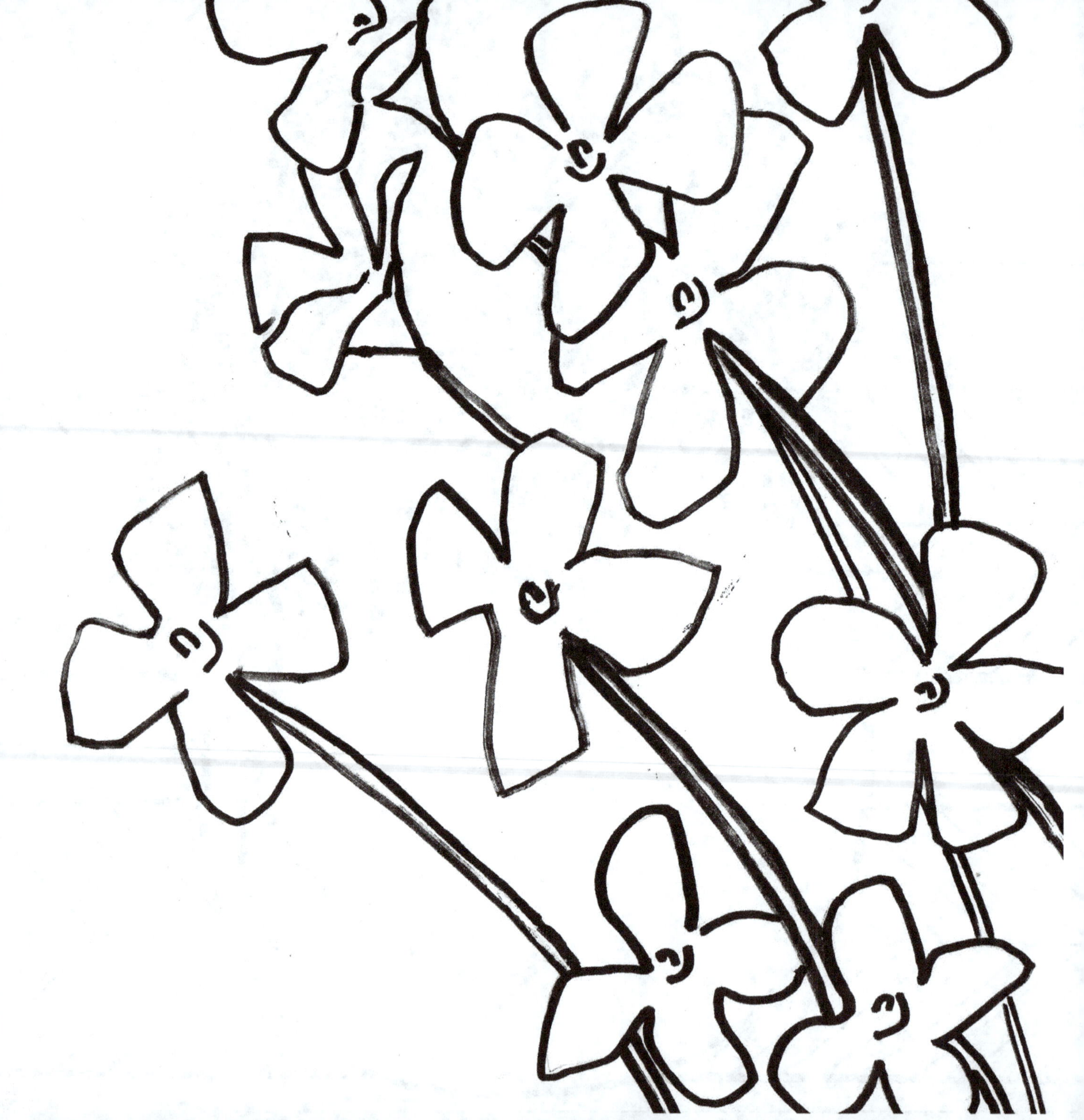

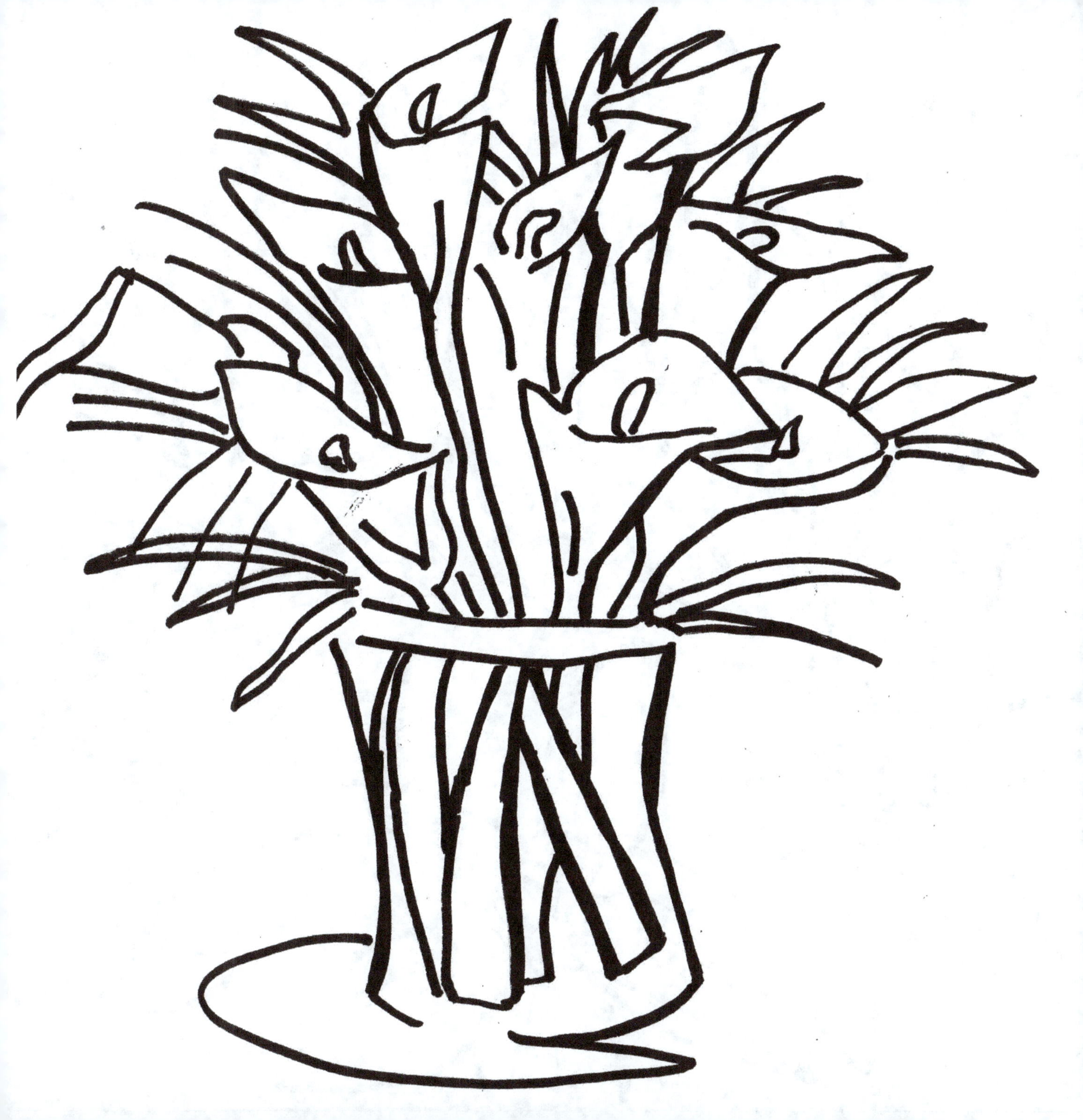

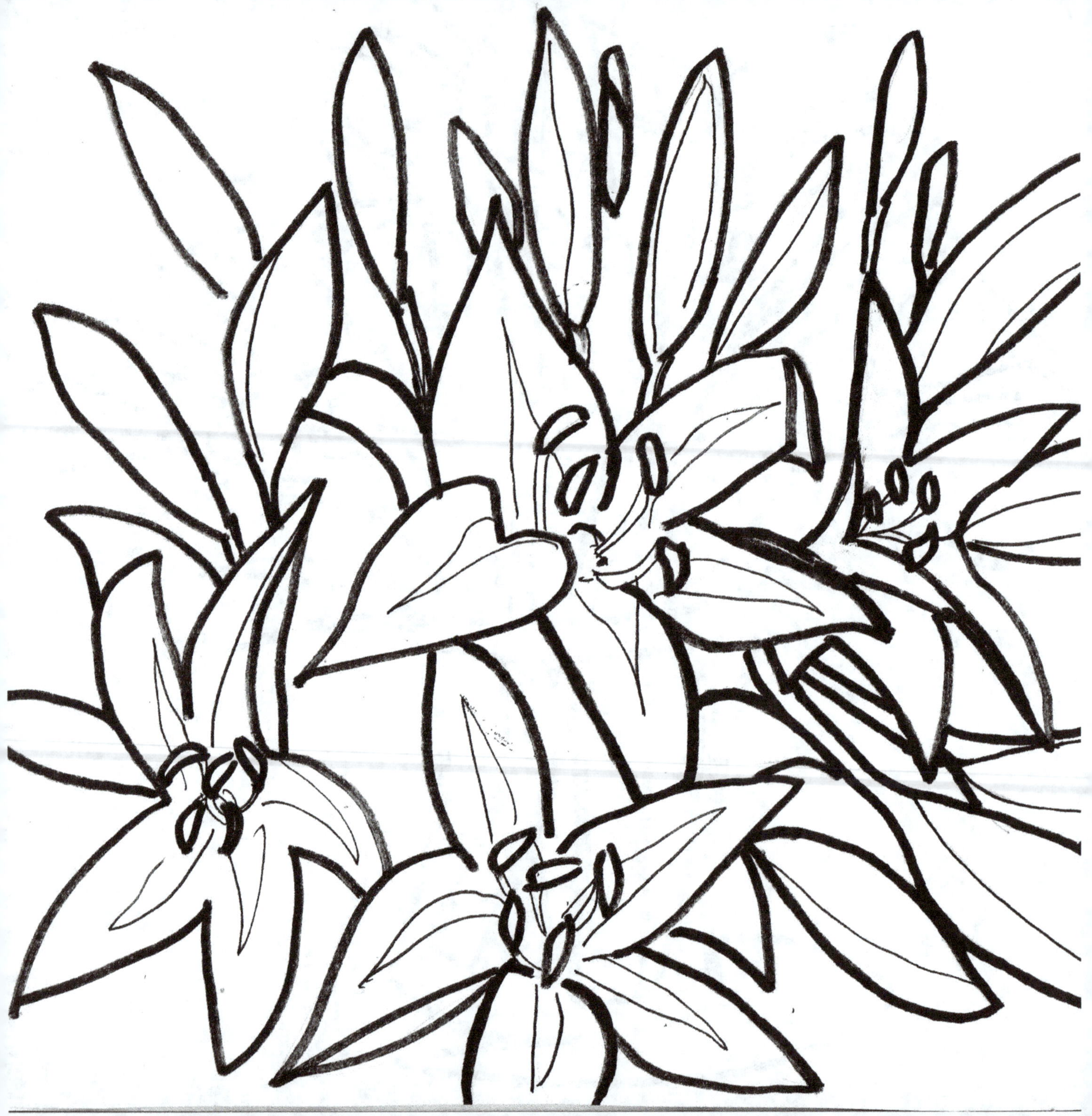

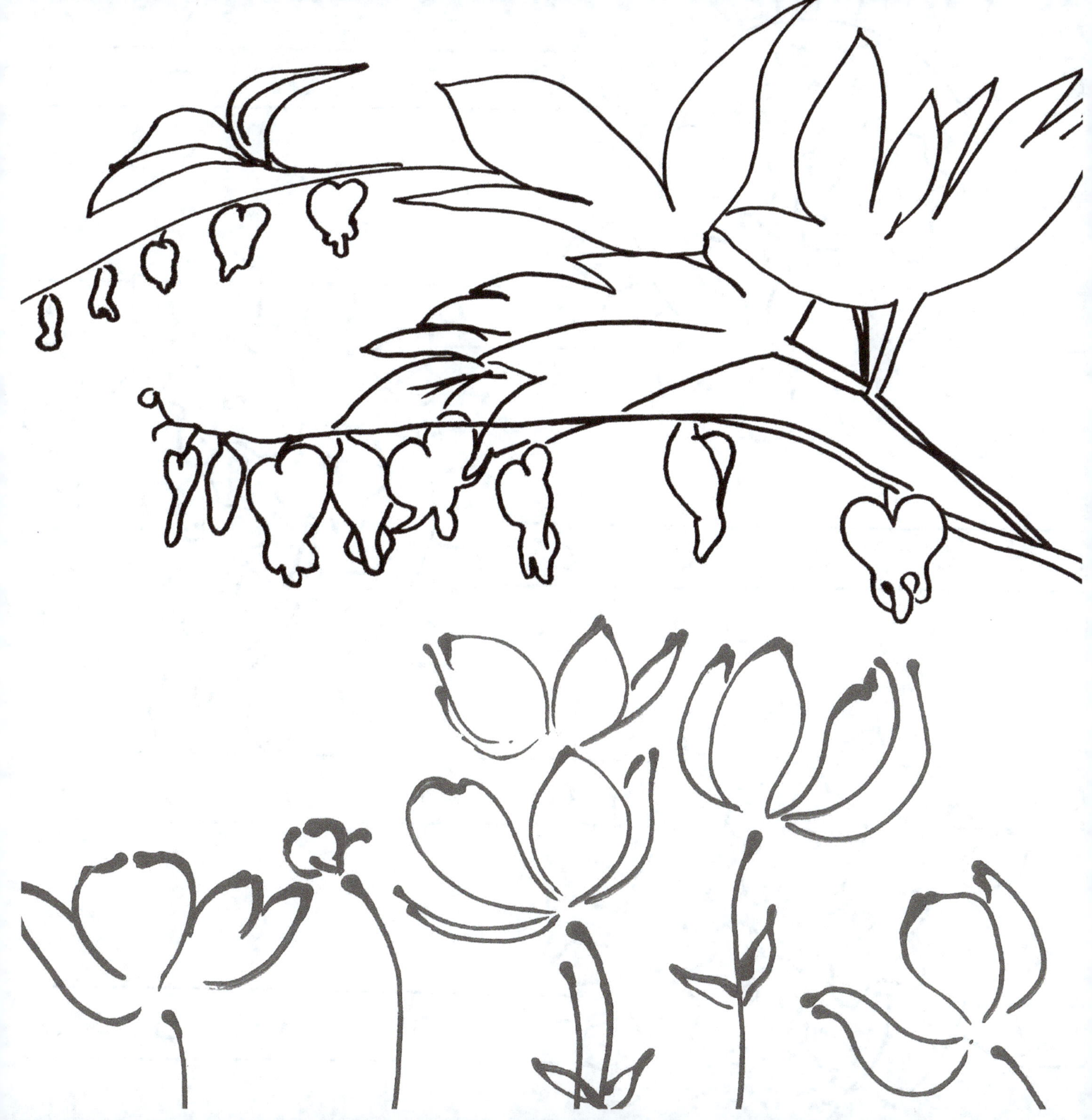

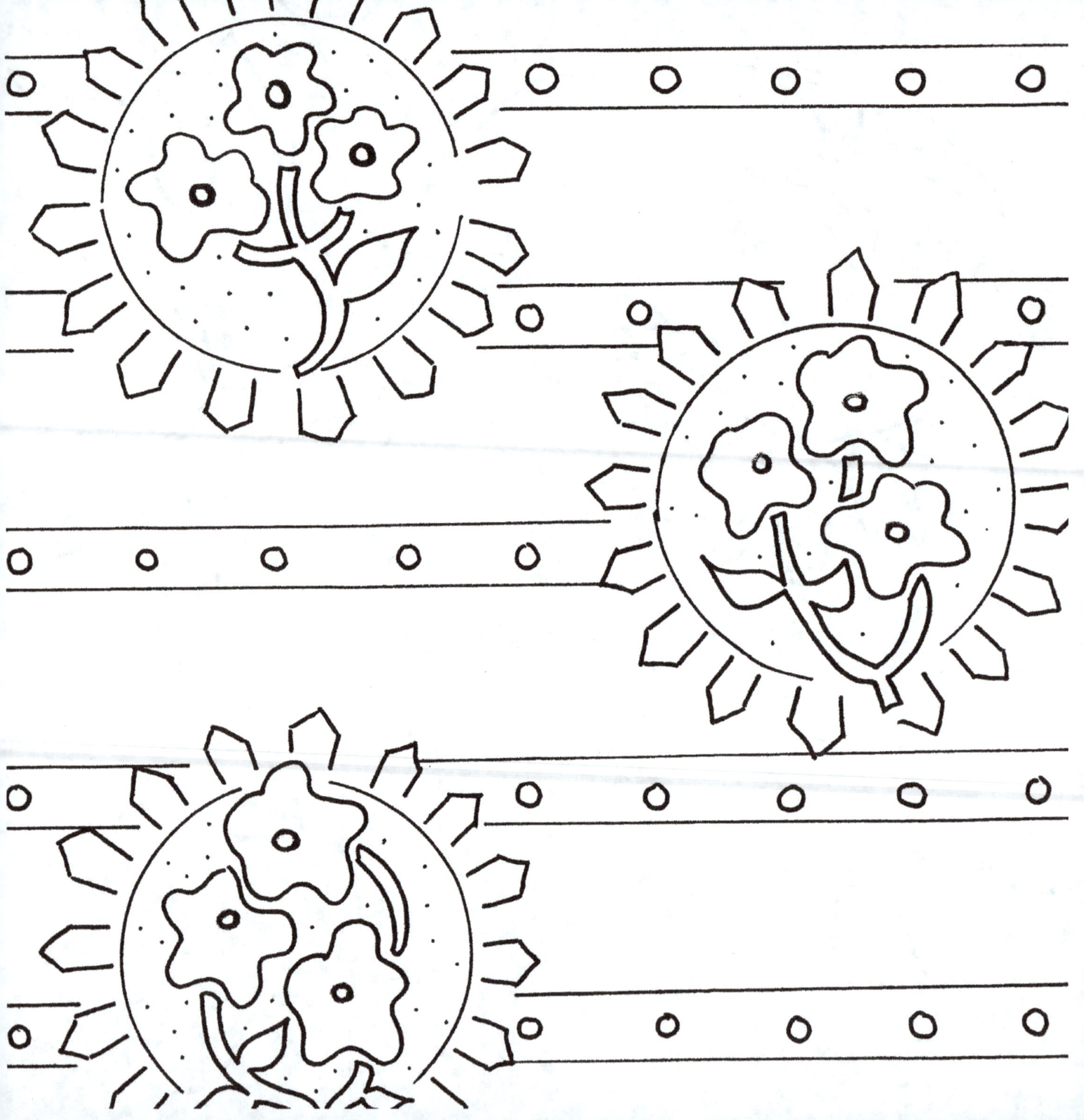

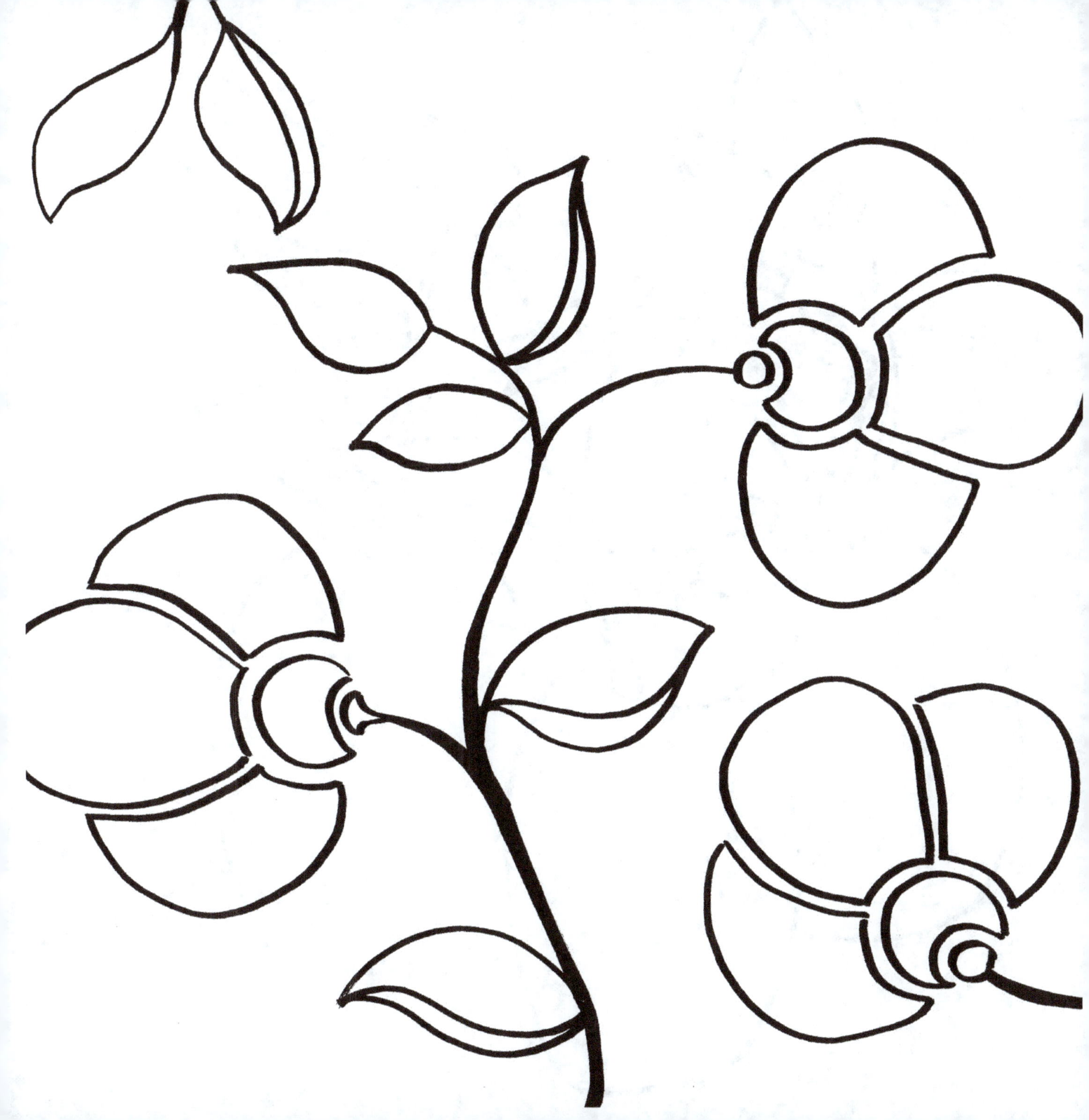

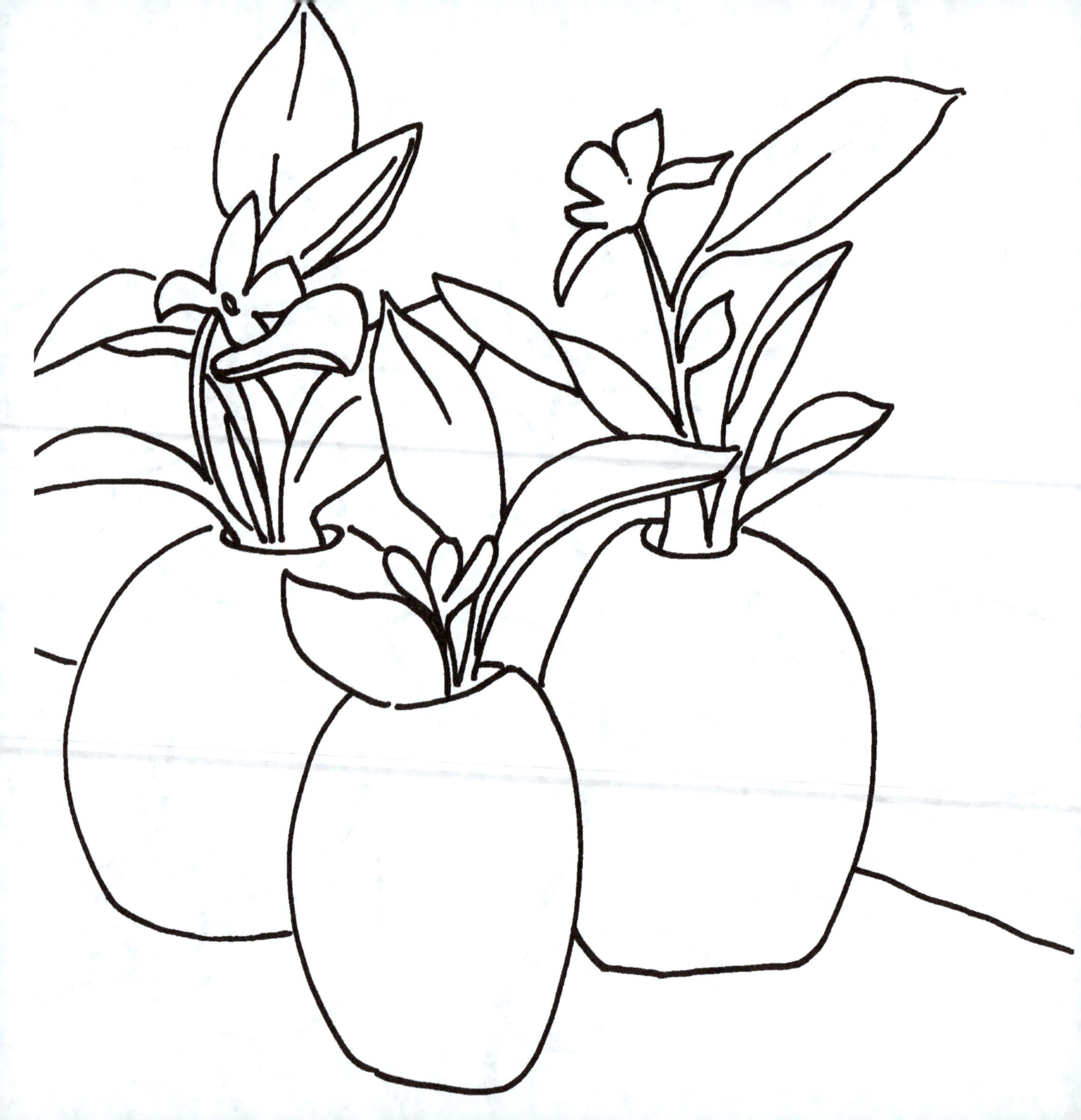

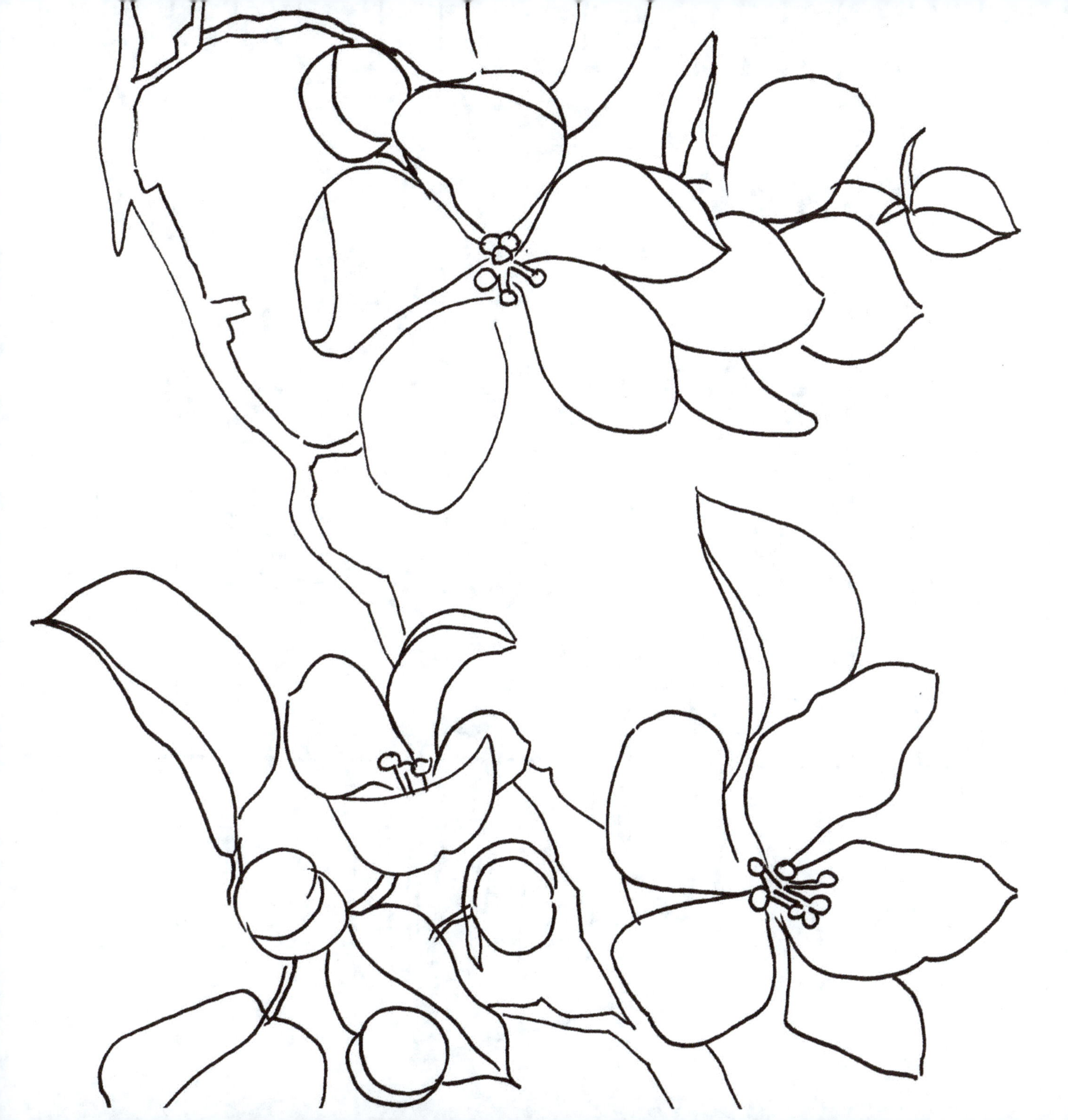

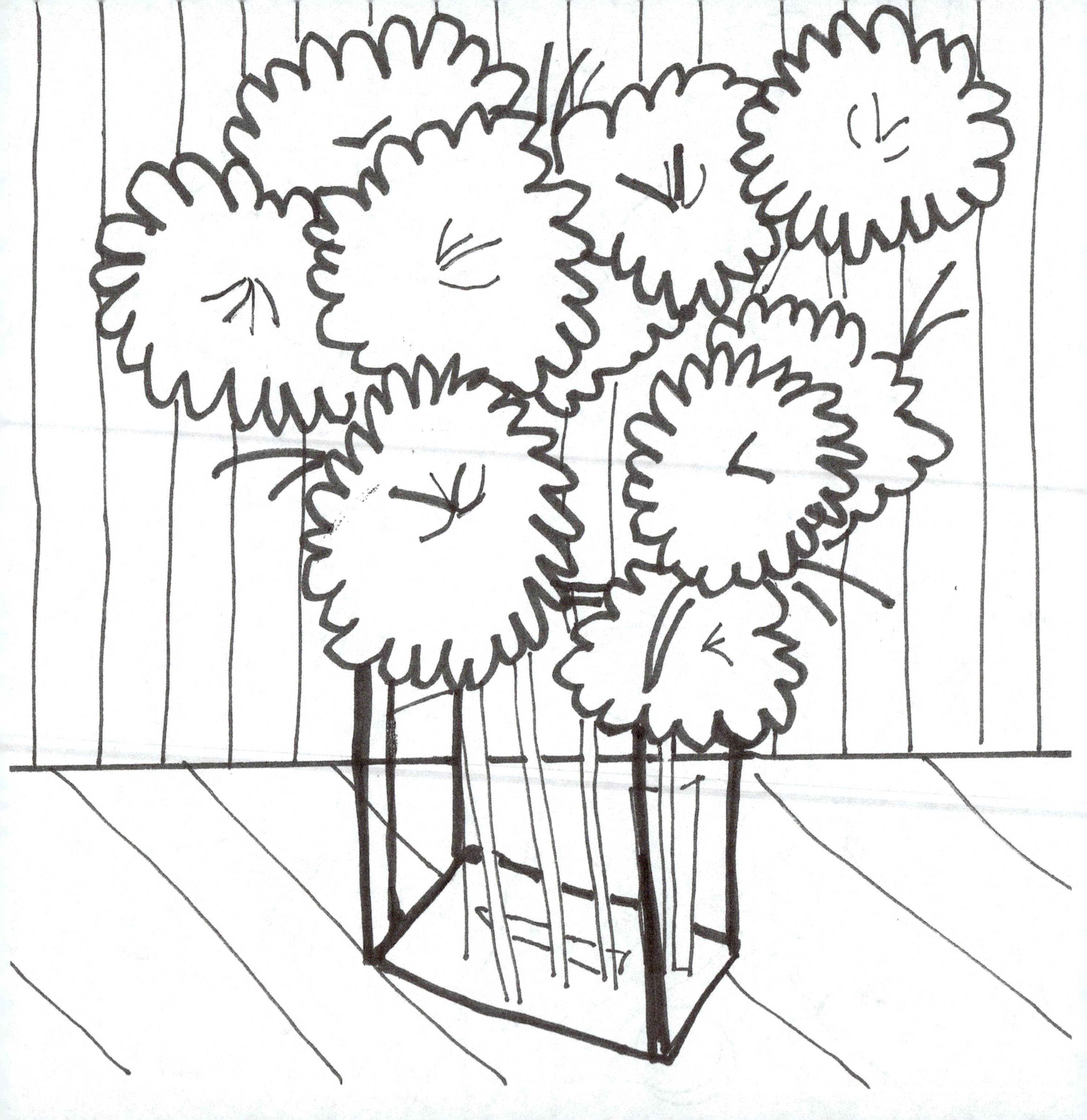

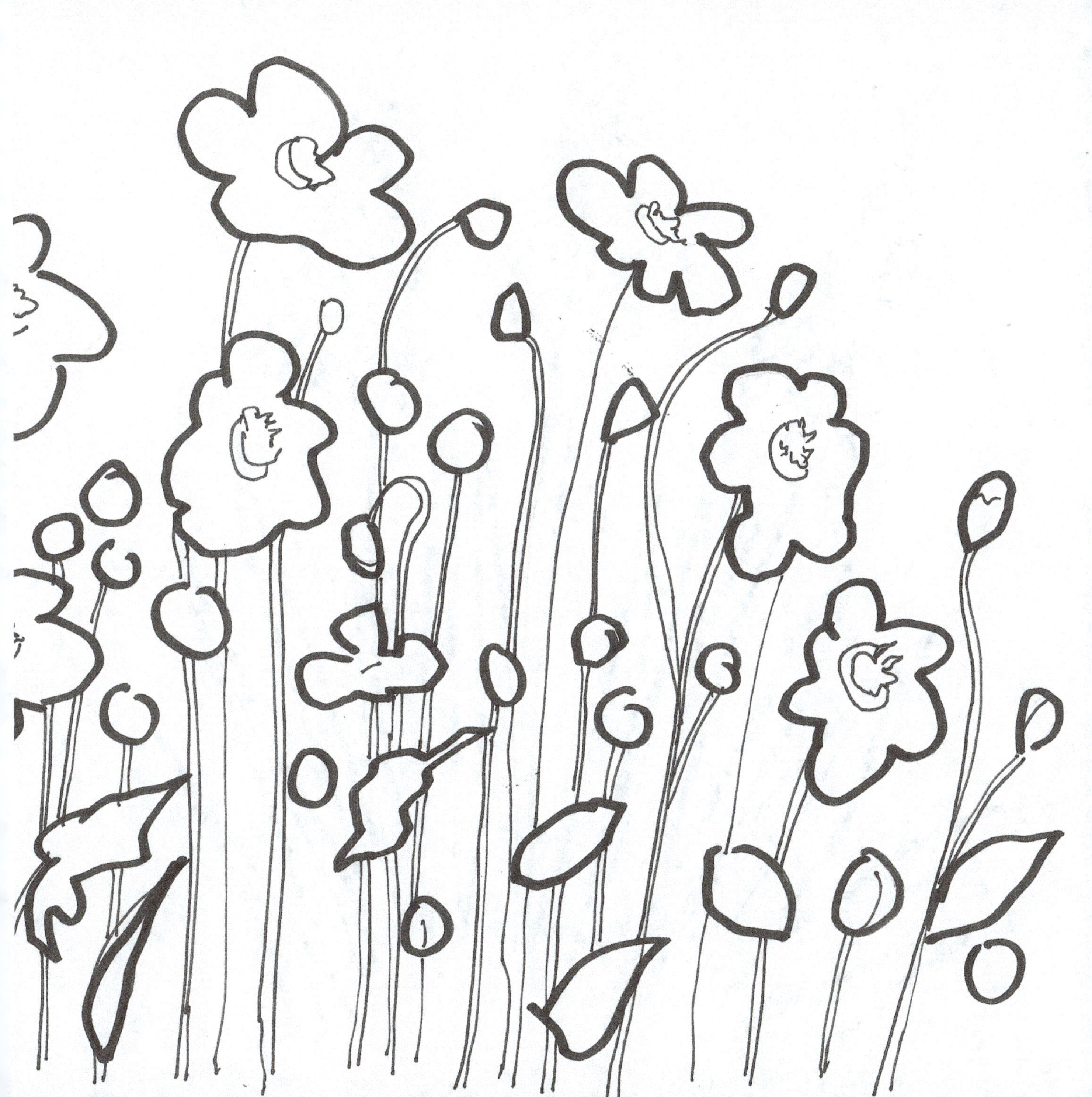

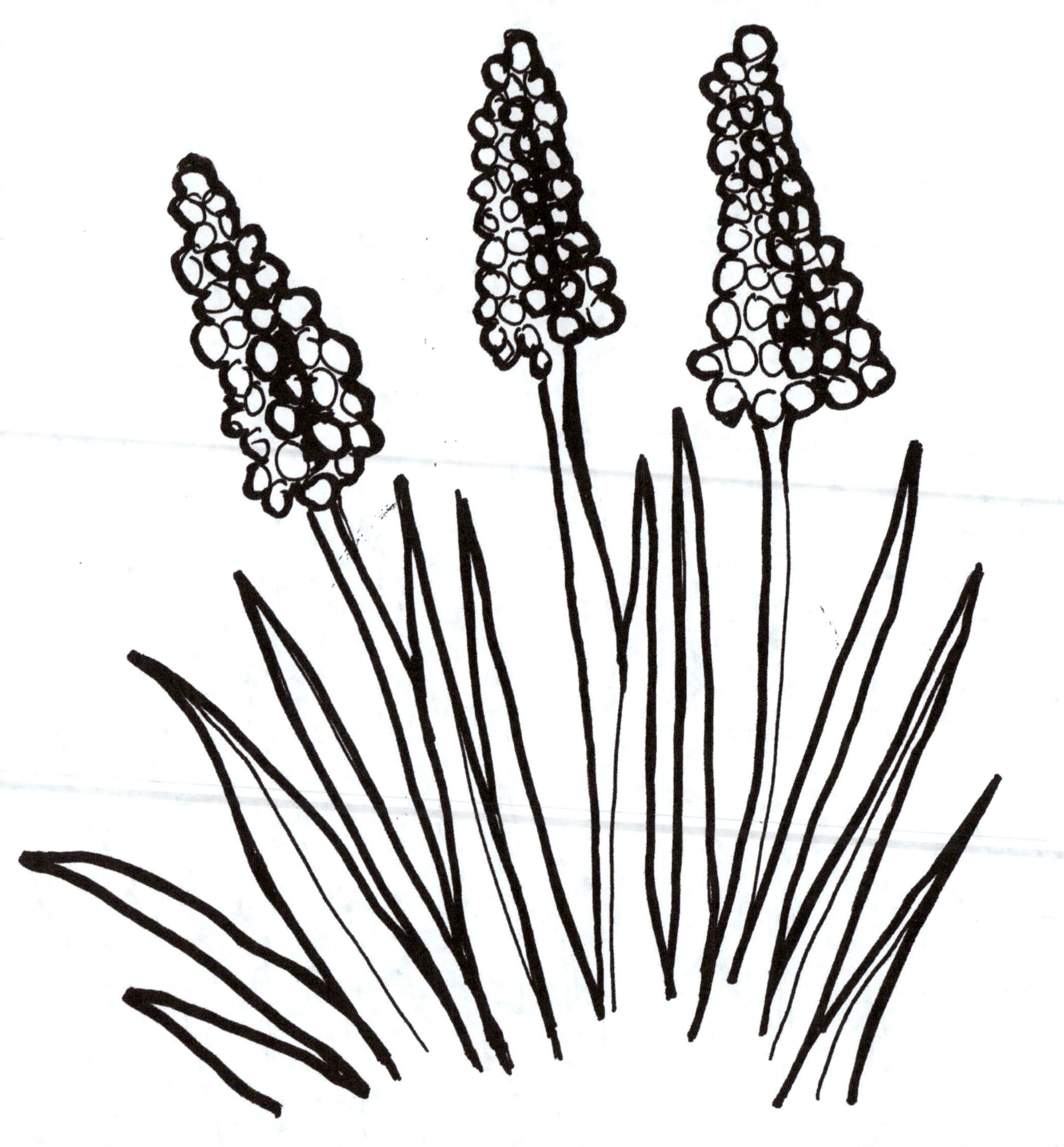

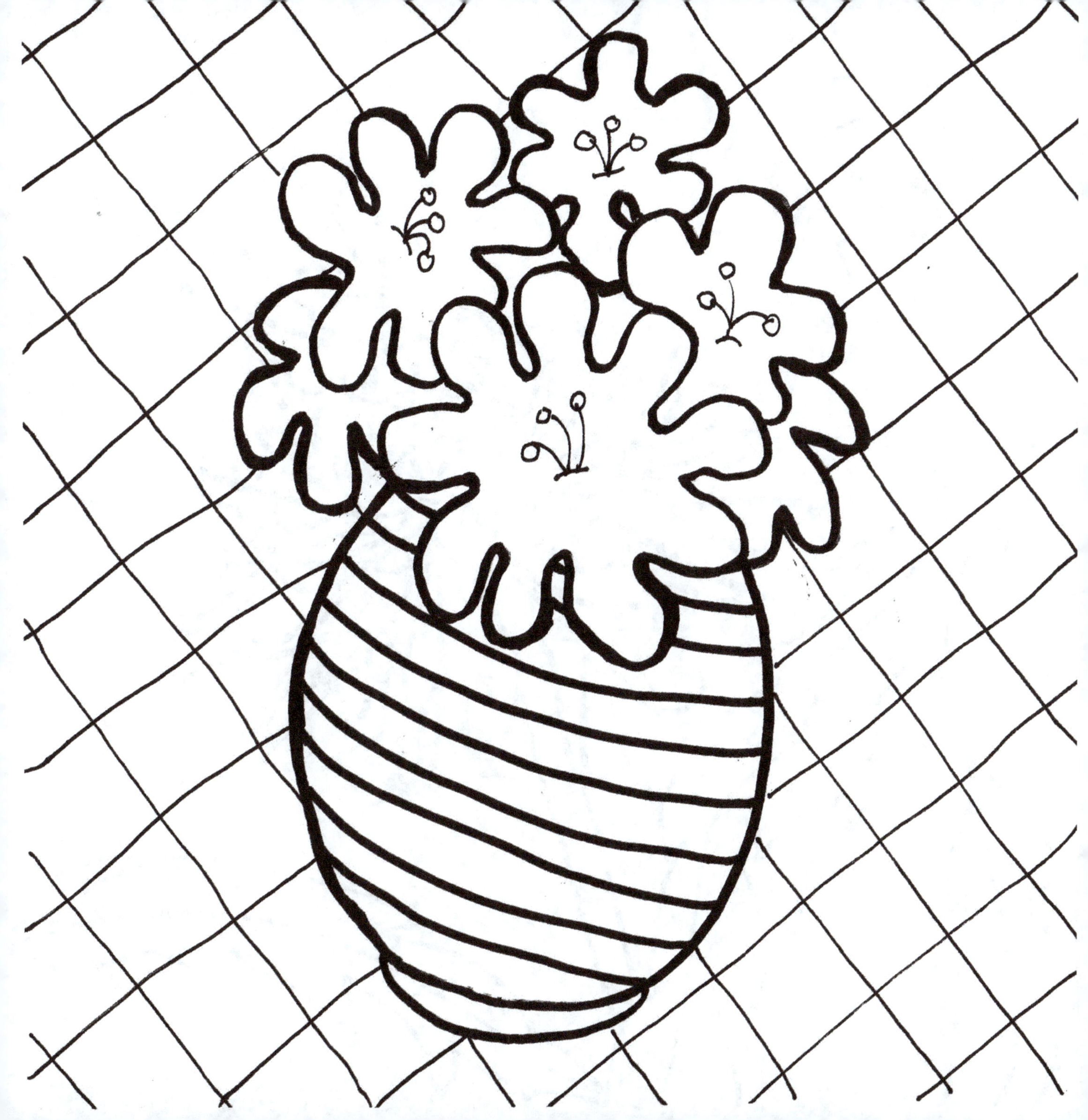

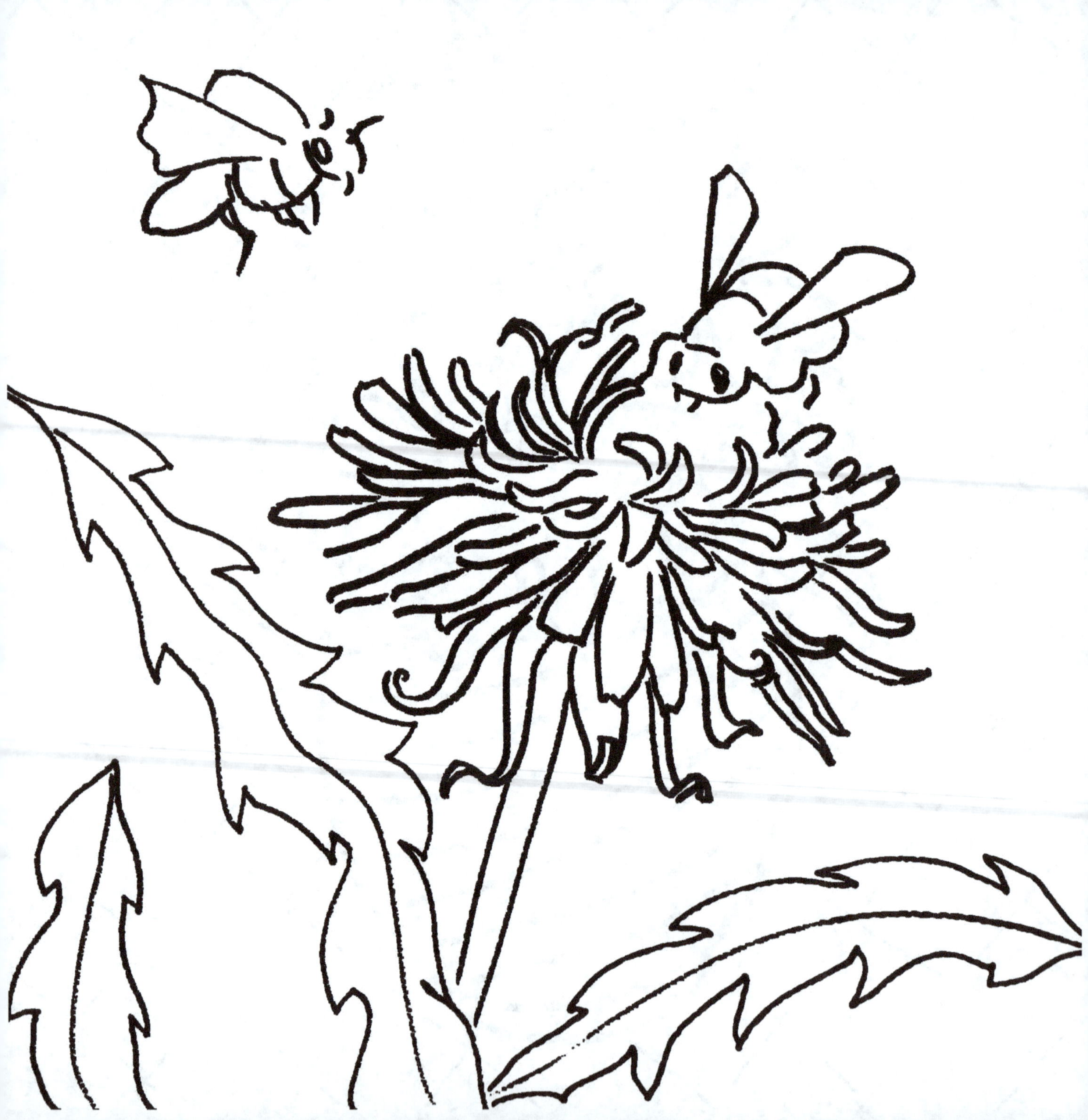

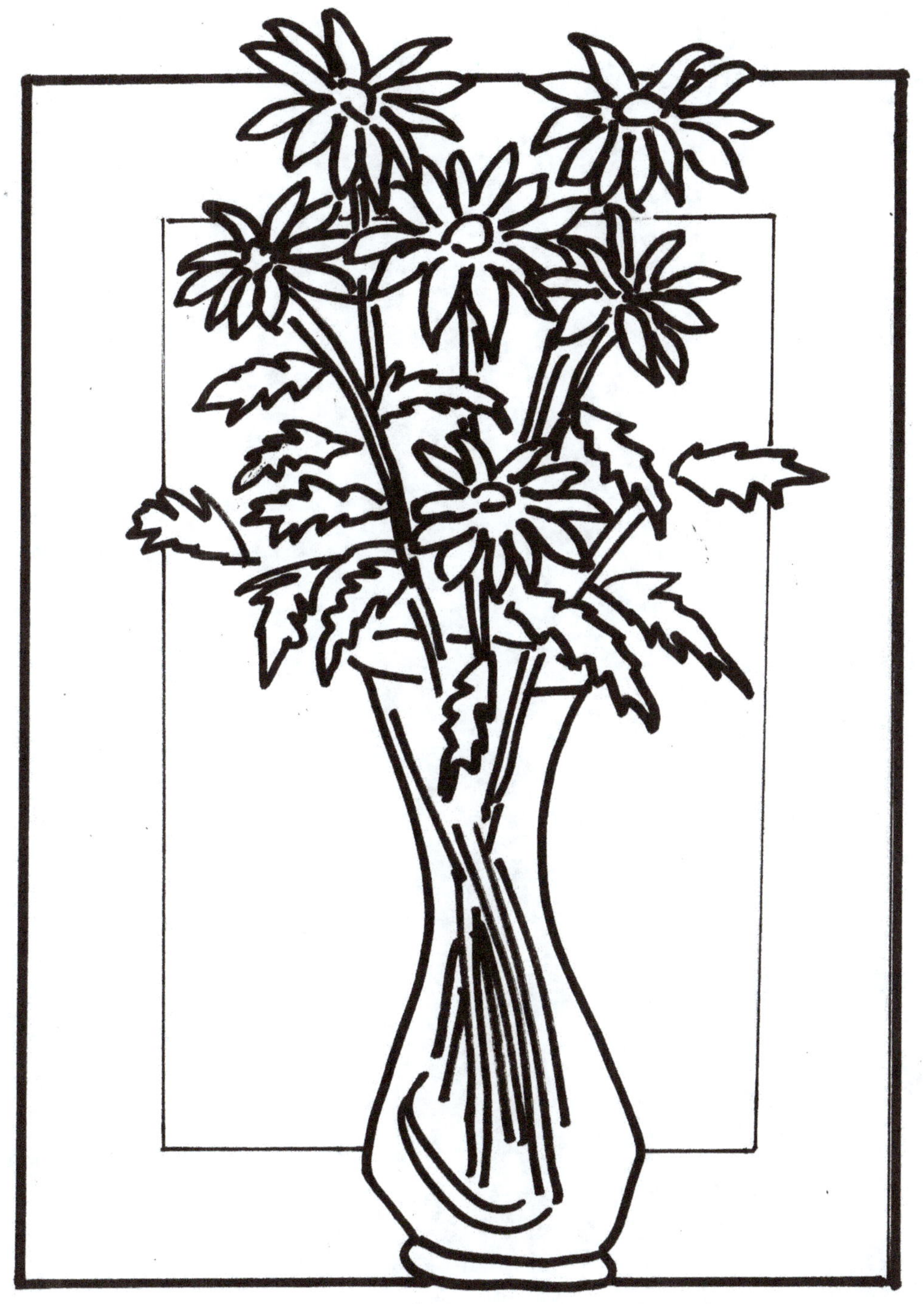

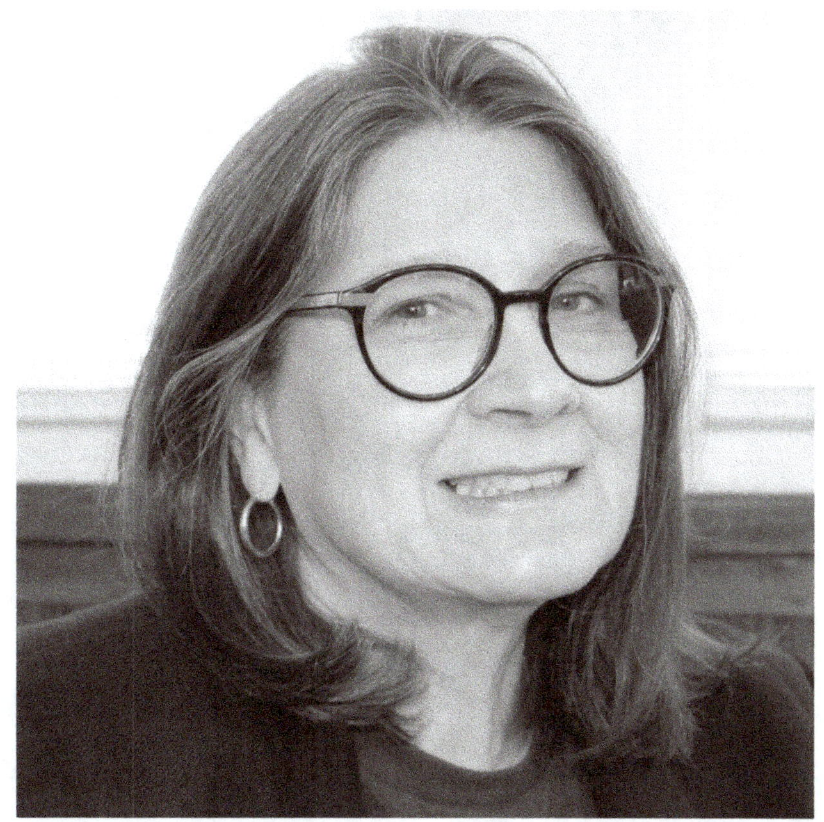

Paula F. Roman-Leon Is a Graphic Designer and Illustrator for over 20 years. She attended Portland School of Art in 1981-1983/renamed Maine College of Art and now lives in Springfield, Virginia. Together, she and Rita Scafidi conducted watercolor workshops with the elderly for 5 years. Paula has worked collectively with other artists in both print and T.V., Books like "Eddy Spaghetti's Birthday" and shows such as Nick Jr.'s "Troll Town", and "Olivia". She is married to Vladimir Roman-Leon for twenty seven years and has 6 children. Paula likes to, cook, paint, draw, listen to music, gardening and strum the ukulele.

Paula F. Roman-Leon 5919 Grayson Street Springfield, VA 22150 703-232-5974 pfgcrl@yahoo.com

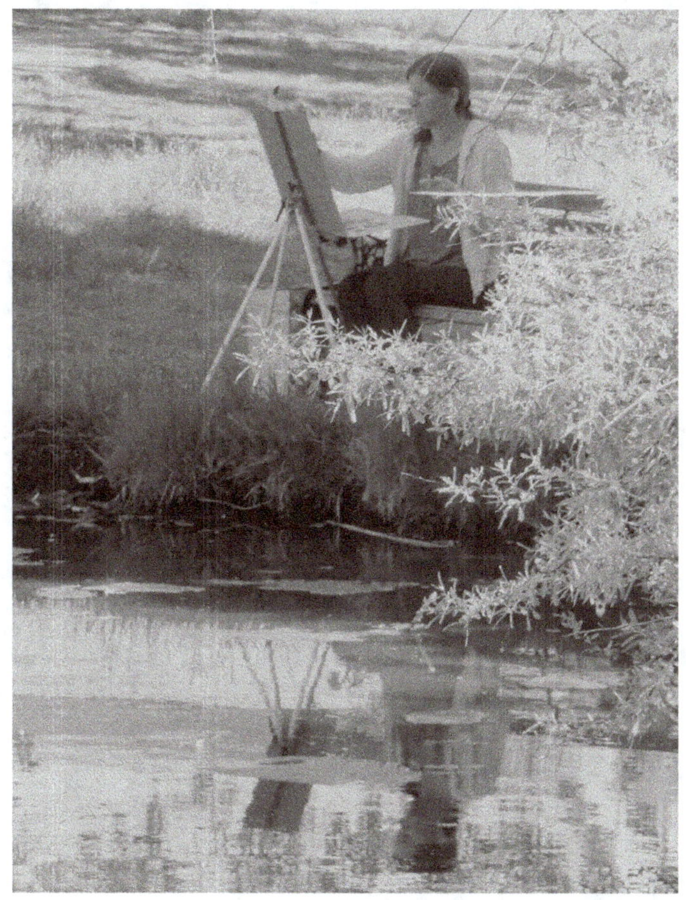

I am thankful to have drawing and painting in my life. The arts are more important than some might realize. When you find yourself involved in one of many creative avenues you will know that it has the ability to bring much learning, excitement, joy and endless possibilities. All of those positives can radiate through you and therefore to those you encounter. I hope you will find that coloring these pages are helpful in giving you the confidence to do some drawings of your own and jump onto this same path that I am so glad to be on. Rita Scafidi

Visit Paula's
Website

at www.pfgcrl.wixsite.com/my-site

for more about her art!

A2Z Press LLC

A2Z Press LLC

published this work.

A2Z Press LLC is a

publishing company

created by Terrie Sizemore

for the purpose

of publishing literary works by new

and aspiring writers. All content is

G-rated. We welcome your submissions

of ideas for children's literature as well

as adult and self-help topics.

Science and medicine, holidays and

other interesting topics are all welcome.

Submit queries to sizemore3630@aol.com or

PO Box 582

Deleon Springs, FL 32130